BILLY JOEL

*an
Illustrated
Biography*

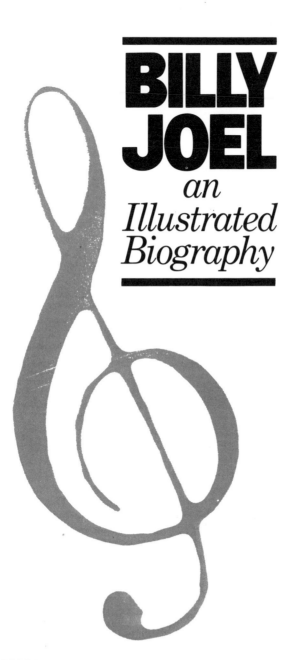

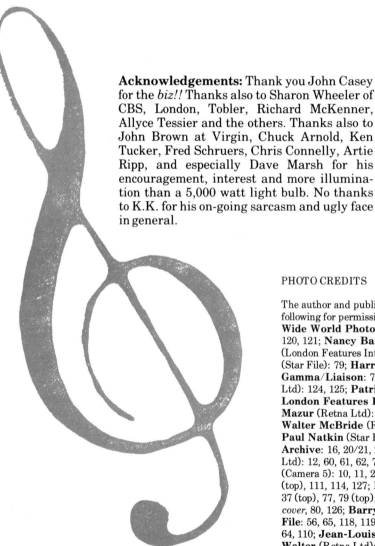

Acknowledgements: Thank you John Casey for the *biz!!* Thanks also to Sharon Wheeler of CBS, London, Tobler, Richard McKenner, Allyce Tessier and the others. Thanks also to John Brown at Virgin, Chuck Arnold, Ken Tucker, Fred Schruers, Chris Connelly, Artie Ripp, and especially Dave Marsh for his encouragement, interest and more illumination than a 5,000 watt light bulb. No thanks to K.K. for his on-going sarcasm and ugly face in general.

BILLY JOEL

an *Illustrated Biography*

BY DEBBIE GELLER AND TOM HIBBERT

McGRAW-HILL BOOK COMPANY
New York · St Louis · San Francisco · Bogotá · Guatemala · Hamburg · Lisbon
Madrid · Mexico · Montreal · Panama · Paris · San Juan
São Paolo · Tokyo · Toronto

1 2 3 4 5 6 7 8 9   8 7 6 5

ISBN 0-07-023055-2

Library of Congress Cataloging in Publication Data

Geller, Debbie.
   Billy Joel.

    1. Joel, Billy. 2. Singers – United States – Biography. 3. Rock musicians – United States – Biography. I. Hibbert, Tom. II. Title.

ML420.**J**72G4   1985   784.5′4′00924   **[B]**   85-4315
ISBN 0-07-023055-2

CONTENTS

1

OFF WE GO TO MUSIC LAND

As kids of the Fifties went, Billy Joel was pretty average: a bright boy and a loving son, a snotty-nosed brat and an apprentice hoodlum; he was fascinated by history and he loved opera, he sniffed glue and fell down drunk in the alley; he'd fret about his machismo, he'd pull idiotic stunts to impress the girls. He was a mixed-up, all-American kid. His head was screwed on the right way. Average. Naturally, he had dreams of being famous. Sometimes.

He was born on 9 May 1949, William Martin Joel, a son for Howard and Rosalind, a brother for Judy. Howard Joël had been born in Nuremburg, Germany, and during the Second World War was imprisoned as a Jew by the Nazis in Dachau's notorious concentration camp. He survived his incarceration and, after the war, left Germany and arrived in America – via Havana, Cuba – to make a new life in New York. He dropped the umlaut from his surname, he secured a well-paid executive job with General Electric, and he married Rosalind Hyman. Howard was a classically trained pianist; Rosalind had been singing in the chorus of a Gilbert and Sul-

❝ *Do you know any average kids? Everybody is totally out of their minds – there's nobody normal. But kids are supposed to be average. They're supposed to be straight ahead and become President of the United States. Well, Richard Nixon got to be President of the United States and he was out of his tree. That's average? OK, then, I'm totally average.* **❞**

Billy Joel, 1979

livan operetta company. After their marriage in the Bronx the couple moved to Hicksville, Long Island, about three blocks away from the Hicksville/ Levittown border, and raised a couple of kids. Average.

Long Island is held in more contempt than almost any other area of the United States. Not even New Jersey (a standing joke until Bruce Springsteen gave it a somewhat romantic aura), or the Midwest, which is merely bland, or the South, which is weird and sometimes exotic, take the knocks that Long Island takes. As Billy Joel has said: "There's an identity crisis. You're a nothing, you're a zero in the suburbs. You're mundane, you're common. You have 2.4 children, you have a quarter acre of land, you have a Ford Wagoneer. Who gives a damn about you?" And if that's how people think about the suburbs, multiply it a thousand times and that's how people think about Levittown, Long Island.

Levittown stands as the prototype for all post-war American suburbs, the kind of anonymous towns that the Cleaver and Stone families lived in. Levittown was built as a residential community in the 1940s as a place for war veterans and their new families – the brood that resulted from all that returning-home lust – to live the good life. Made from prefabricated parts in an assembly line fashion that rivalled Ford, the more than 17,000 homes that made up the town had been finished by 1951 and were occupied post-haste.

With its tract housing, dull landscaping, ghetto-without-the-tenements crowding, Levittown was, if anything, a waiting-room *en route* to real affluence. The streets, with such whimsical names as Memory Lane, Spindle Road, Kingfisher Road and Horn Lane, were planned into meandering swirls and twists in an attempt to confound the monotony. The houses came in two styles – "Cape Cod" and "Ranch". Average. Average and all the same. But Billy Joel remains proud of his hometown; he'll defend Levittown to the death. "Oh, you're from the sub-urbs!" he'll ooze with a mixture of contempt and pith in one of his imitations of a mellow, laid-back, new-age Californian. "Ooooooh, what a drag. . .Well . . ." – back to his own New York tough tones – "I had a good time. . ."

"I was a real pain in the neck as a kid. I had a lot of energy and I was always banging on that piano . . ."

When Joel Sr. was at home (which wasn't often – he was frequently away on business trips) he would tinker about on the family's "crappy" old Lester upright. "The piano had been painted 50,000 times and was rusty and everything," Billy later recalled. "But he would make it sound pretty. I loved to hear him play. He'd play nocturnes and Bartok." Billy's own touch on the piano was rather less subtle in those days: "I was a real pain in the neck as a kid. I had a lot of energy and I was always banging on that piano, beating the hell out of it." The boy also thought it quite amusing to pour lighter fluid on the keys and set them ablaze with a match; when he was four, Rosalind decided it was time her son put his surplus energy to constructive use so she

hauled him off to piano lessons with a Miss Francis who lived down the street. "I was forced into it," Joel remembers. "My arm was twisted and I was marched off down the block. It was real humiliating because Miss Francis also taught ballet."

Miss Francis put her new charge to work on the John Thompson Piano Tutor Volume I, a book jam-packed with weedy little tunes:

"The first song I ever learned was 'Off We Go To Music Land'. It was really simple and I started riffing on it right away."

"Anybody that takes piano lessons must know about the John Thompson books – every song has a title like 'The Strong Man' or 'The Swan' and the first song I ever learned was 'Off We Go To Music Land'. It was really simple and I started riffing on it right away." Though Billy hated his lessons – the practice, the theory and technique – he soon found he had a natural inclination for the instrument and he would sit at home at the Lester getting kicks from his own improvisations. His irreverent approach to the classics exasperated his father: "I had a Beethoven piece – one of the sonatas – and I started boogie-woogieing to it one day. My old man came downstairs and smacked the hell out of me." (Howard Joel never did come to terms with rock'n'roll music: "My father's a really good piano player," says the son. "I won't play in front of him – he's *real* good. And he's like 'Jeez! I play piano better than him. So how come *he's* making all that money?' He's confused by the whole thing.")

In 1957, the Joels were divorced and Howard returned to Europe, eventually settling in Vienna where he continued to work for General Electric. Up until then, life had been pretty comfortable but now Rosalind was forced out to work as a secretary and book-keeper. "It was a real bummer," Billy would recall years later, adding with characteristic exaggeration: "It was traumatic not having food sometimes." Money was tight but not *that* tight; the rented TV set might have been taken away but there was always enough to pay for the piano lessons and for the occasional highbrow outing to New York City – to the opera or the sissy ballet: "I got a lot of culture because Mom enjoyed it and wanted to pass it along. Plus, she saw I had a talent for it, so she was going to kick my ass."

While Rosalind looked after the meals and the culture, her father Philip Hyman became something of a paternal figure for her two children: "He was the most inspiring figure in my life," Billy would say.

Hyman, an Englishman from a Jewish family of tinsmiths, had fought with the Loyalists, in the Abraham Lincoln Brigade, against Franco's forces in the Spanish Civil War and was branded a Communist during the McCarthy hearings of the early Fifties. He worked as a jeweller but hardly made a bean: "He didn't have a dime because all his energies were funnelled into the pursuit of knowledge. He used to sit in bed at night and read books on trigonometry and paleantology. He didn't respect anything but knowledge. He was the only self-fulfilled soul I've ever known." It was Hyman's influence that turned Billy into a "history nut" and a voracious reader: "I read everything. I used to read history books like they were novels – anything I could get my hands on. A lot of my romanticism comes from novelists like F.Scott Fitzgerald, Ernest Hemingway, Mark Twain, Sartre, Kafka, Hesse." And it was Hyman who taught Billy to question religion and come to the conclusion that it was, on the whole, just a lot of "very enthralling hocus-pocus."

Joel's religious upbringing, such as it was, was confused; Billy's father was a Jew but Billy wasn't raised a Jew; Billy grew up in a predominantly Catholic neighbourhood but he wasn't raised a Catholic, though he *did* go to Mass with his friends because it seemed like a normal and sociable thing to do. "We were the gypsy family," he has said, "the only family where there had been a divorce, the only one that wasn't Catholic, the only one without a driveway. Everybody had the same house so they'd try to make theirs different by fancying up the driveway or painting the trim different." Rosalind Joel didn't have ample funds for such modernisations – but if Billy's house was going to look different, at least his Sundays were going to be the same as anyone else's. So he went to Mass and he'd go to confession too and roll off lists of disgusting acts of invented sin to shock the priests for a lark. For a while, Rosalind took her children to an Evangelical church, the Church of Jesus Christ, and Billy was baptised there when he was 12. However, at a subsequent service the preacher held up a dollar bill and proclaimed it "the flag of the Jews". The Joels quit Evangelicalism after that. Billy was beginning to think that the whole religious trip was a trifle absurd: "It was interesting observing the effect religious guilt had on people, especially women. Jewish guilt is very visceral. It goes right to the guts, it's physical. Catholic guilt is very gothic – cathedrals of the mind with bats flying and incense. It can be very devastating. Guys were always like 'Hey, it's OK. Just don't get anybody pregnant and don't bring the cops home.' But with girls it was like 'Don't do *anything* or you'll burn in hell for the rest of your life!' "

He was short and snub-nosed and the girls never gave him a second glance – until One Day In The Gymnasium.

None of the girls in school seemed in much danger of being condemned to eternal damnation – not for misbehaving with the prepubescent BJ at any rate. For he was not the most prepossessing of brats: he was in the choir which was kind of "faggy", he read books which was kind of "spooky", he was short and snub-nosed and the girls never gave him a second glance – until One Day In The Gymnasium.

After lunch at Fork Lane School, the kids would spend half an hour in the gym goofing around, dancing, singing and generally acting up. And one such afternoon, when Billy was in 4th grade, he suddenly got the urge to leap on to the gymnasium stage and launch into an unrehearsed, unaccompanied version of Elvis Presley's 'Hound Dog': "I was shaking my hips and jiggling like Elvis – and when you're eleven years old you don't even *have* hips. But the girls in the 6th grade started screaming and the teacher pulled me off stage like I was doing something obscene." Billy Joel's albeit short debut stage appearance had been an unqualified hit.

Up until now, Billy hadn't been particularly interested in rock 'n' roll. As his piano playing developed, he'd started listening to jazz – Bill Evans, Oscar Peterson, Art Tatum – and his attitude to rock was somewhat toffee-nosed and snooty – he considered most of it "horrible and embarrassing." His sister used to carry around a record tote case, with "I Love Boys" embossed on the side, stuffed with 45s which she'd play on her "junky" record-player – Fabian and all the other smartly-groomed dreamboats with gleaming teeth didn't impress Billy one little bit. But those screams in the gymnasium had intrigued him.

In 1962, Billy saw live rock music for the first time when he took a train with a couple of friends to Harlem where James Brown and the Fabulous Flames were playing at the Apollo Theatre. Once inside, the three boys from Hicksville became scared – they were the only white kids in the building and some of the looks they were getting were unnerving. They were about to sneak out – but then the show began, Brown came on stage and they were transfixed: "He'd put his cape on and he'd walk off the stage and they'd drag him on again and he did the greatest footwork I ever saw. He'd move all across the stage on one foot and he'd come back the other way on the other foot. It wasn't very sophisticated and the compositions were fairly primitive but the performance just knocked the *hell* out of me.

"Pop music didn't hit me until then – James Brown, the Phil Spector records, Sam and Dave, Wilson Pickett, Otis Redding – that was the first music I *felt*. There was passion in it." He started tuning in to New York's R&B radio stations; he played interpretations of what he heard on the piano; he went to further concerts – like The Temptations at Palisades Park in New Jersey: "They got on stage and just lip-synched to a record. I couldn't believe they were doing this but the audience just ate it up. I had to hand it to them."

Meanwhile, now well into adolescence, Billy had joined a gang of street urchins, the Parkway Green Gang, and was living out a

low-life fantasy as a snot-rich hoodlum punk. There would be no more taunts and gibes from uncouth Polish kids as he made his way back from piano class with his "faggy" music books under his arm. Because nobody messed with the Parkway Green Gang on the Parkway Green Gang's turf. Or so the Parkway Green Gang liked to believe. . .

Levittown wasn't the South Bronx or anything. There wasn't enough poverty to produce the random kind of violence that decaying inner cities can cough up. The rough antics of Levittown's youth never made the nightly news. Girls teased their hair and wore lots of make-up, black stockings (with holes they fixed with nail polish) and Beatle-style boots. Guys, according to Billy's high school music teacher, wore jeans, leather jackets and engineer boots. But most of the kids who walked down the streets in packs, wearing matching jackets and snapping their fingers in time to the tunes they were harmonising, didn't grow up to do time in the pen. Instead, they became accountants, teachers and civil servants like their fathers before them.

The Parkway Green Gang members had all seen *West Side Story* and had been seduced by the film's teen mob glamour. They borrowed the "heavy, heavy honour code" of The Sharks (or was it The Jets?) and they borrowed the movie gangs' dress codes too, togging up in leather jackets, purple shirts, chino pants and Astro boots with stupid little space rocket motifs on the sides. If you were cool, you ripped the rockets off. "I still get choked up when I see *West Side Story*," Billy Joel confessed years after his gangland days. "It sounds dopey but I get mushy about it. It's real mushy." And pretty "mushy", rather than mean and malevolent, is pretty much what the Parkway Green Gang was; they were hardly the scariest, baddest collection of disaffected toughs ever to stalk suburban streets. They were too busy guzzling Tango wine, sniffing glue and playing bombed-out versions of chicken, running across boards 30 feet above the parkway – if you slipped, you got squashed, haw, haw, haw – to really frighten anyone much apart from themselves. Mental macho. As Joel has admitted, they were just *trying* to look tough: "We weren't nearly as tough as we thought we were."

To prove how tough he thought *he* was, Billy took up boxing when he was 16, joining a programme at a police-sponsored boys club in Mid-Island Shopping Plaza, Hicksville. "I must have been out of my mind because boxing is very violent and brutal. But I got my whole male-identity crisis out of the way in those three years of boxing." He was pretty good at it, too. He won 21 bouts out of 25 before coming up against a gorilla: "This guy's arms were the size of my entire body. . . he got me with a left hook. Boom! I went right down. I could have gotten up but I decided to hell with it, who needs this?"

In the dressing-room after the fight, Billy glanced in a mirror and was perturbed to see that his nose was all swollen and resting at a peculiar angle to his face. A helpful fellow club member came up and pushed the misaligned organ back into position. Joel's nose was never the same after that. "It never healed right and now I've got two different-sized nostrils. I thought about getting it fixed but I was worried it would change my voice." For by now Billy Joel was singing in a rock band and making a living from music. . .

2

WHO'S THAT BANGING ON THE PIANO?

On 9 February 1964, The Beatles arrived at CBS TV studios on New York's 53rd Street to rehearse for their first US TV appearance on The Ed Sullivan Show. Outside the building a young man paced the sidewalk bearing a placard that read: "Alonzo Tuske Hates The Beatles". Alonzo Tuske's protest against cheap English imports was as futile as it was lonely. The fabulous Mop Tops were about to change the face of almost everything; one of the greatest conversational clichés of the Sixties – one to rival "Where were *you* when President Kennedy was assassinated?" – was about to be born. "Where were YOU the night The Beatles played on The Ed Sullivan Show?"

Billy Joel was at a friend's house glued to a TV set, stunned. "They were *mine*. They didn't look like Fabian. They looked like me and my friends. Man, *I* could do that. I could *try* to do that, anyway."

Suddenly there were these four guys who didn't look like puppets created by Hollywood. They were real people. They were sort of wise-ass and they were singing songs they'd written themselves. McCartney looked pretty cute but the rest were just street guys. And Lennon had this look in his eye. I thought 'That's pretty cool!'

Billy Joel, 1984

And try he did. The Beatles and the British invasion rendered New York's existing music scene obsolete almost overnight. Suddenly it had become necessary to sport fringes and Chelsea boots and, if possible, feign a Liverpool or Cockney accent if you were to cut the mustard as a pop act. On every street in every suburb, there was a scuzzy garage band twanging away hopefully in the new tradition. One of Long Island's many would-be beat phenomena was a teenage group called The Echoes. Early in 1964, they approached Joel at Hicksville Junior High and asked him to join. "I couldn't figure out why they wanted me. Everybody was playing guitars and I didn't know where a piano would fit in. We used to stick a microphone in the back of the piano – a Kent microphone, real piece of garbage – and we were all plugged into one amplifier. It was a Magnitone amp and it had this little reverb

13

chamber and we turned it all the way up and thought we were The Righteous Brothers or something. We were pretty lousy, I guess. But I'd kind of given up the idea of being Victor Horowitz."

Initially, The Echoes don't seem to have been much good at aping British beat. They didn't sing and their material was drawn not from Liverpool or London but from California: they did surfing songs like The Surfaris' 'Wipe Out', they did flitty Ventures instrumentals such as 'Perfidia' and 'Walk Don't Run'. They *even* did 'Woolly Bully'. Despite these artistic shortcomings, the group soon landed its first gig at a local church. And after the set, each member got paid something like four dollars. Billy Joel could not believe this. For standing on stage, pretending to be something like a Beatle and having fun, you actually get *paid money?* "That was it. I really didn't have any choice after that. I was a musician."

Eventually The Echoes got themselves some snazzy blue jackets with velvet collars and ditched the instrumental stuff in favour of The Rolling Stones, some Pretty Things, some Dave Clark Five and The Zombies' 'She's Not There', an obligatory number for any self-respecting beatsters by the end of 1964. Billy began to do singing – he had the best voice – and he provided the instrumental interest with his new Estey organ, "one of those little wooden things with air blowing through it. It sounded like a big harmonica only more horrible than that. But when I got it I thought it was the hottest thing ever."

The Estey, with the old Kent microphone stuck down the back, didn't seem to make an awful lot of noise, however, so Joel traded it in for a Vox Continental which "looked great and sounded dinky as hell – just like The Dave Clark Five's."

Billy even started to compose his own material now; his songs were hardly original – "they sounded like ersatz Beatles songs." They were songs with titles like 'Now That She Is Gone' (which contained the timeless lyric "Now that she is gone, I just sit and cry"), 'Journey's End' (containing the even more timeless lyric "I'd climb the highest mountain, And I'd swim the deepest sea") and 'Just Another Lie' (whose lyric is buried in the shifting sands of time). But they were a start.

Listening to The Echoes live on stage in the Teen Canteen at Hicksville High, girls would almost swoon to the slushy teen balladry and almost frug to the beat and the R&B. The Echoes were pretty useless but even then it was evident that the work of Miss Francis, John Thompson *et al* was paying off. Joel, still in his mid-teens, was developing into a deft and articulate instrumentalist, spicing up the drab beat noise with speedy, flashy flourishes that did not always fit the mood of the music but sounded pretty impressive nonetheless.

Listening to The Echoes live on stage in the Teen Canteen at Hicksville High, girls would almost swoon to the slushy teen balladry and almost frug to the beat and the R&B.

The reputation of the flashy organ-playing kid in The Echoes spread and, in the autumn of 1964, he entered a recording studio for the first time: "These two brothers had a tiny studio in a basement and someone asked me to come and play the piano on some session. Nobody knew what the hell it was gonna be." "Nobody" is about right. The session turned out to be a pop scam engineered by eccentric Long Island would-be writer/producer George "Shadow" Morton who had hired Joe Monaco's studio for the day and asked a friend, George Stermer, to pick up some cheap musicians.

Morton hadn't written or produced anything before and, on the way to the studio, something occurred to him, as he recalled in Alan Betrock's 1982 book *Girl Groups: The Story Of A Sound*: "As I crossed the railroad tracks, it dawned on me. . .I didn't have a song. So I pulled the car over and wrote one. . .But then when I walked into the studio, I didn't know how the arrangement went because it was all in my head and I don't play an instrument or anything. So I said to the piano player: 'You play bom, bom, bom. . .' Within two hours we had it done." That piano player was Billy Joel and, once the voices of some girls from Long Island – Mary and Betty Weiss, and Marge and Mary Ann Ganser –

had been overdubbed, and some seagull noises had been stuck on, Morton had a smash hit record – and a pop classic – on his hands: 'Remember (Walking In The Sand)' by The Shangri-Las. (By a spooky quirk of coincidence, a pop adventurer named Artie Ripp owned a little piece of the Shangri-Las and received a production credit on the single; Ripp would emerge later as Joel's producer – and nemesis.)

But *was* that piano player Billy Joel? No one is absolutely sure, least of all Billy himself: "Shadow would sail into the studio with this big cape and his dark glasses – 'Hey, man, I'm Shadow Morton. How ya doin'? What's happenin' here? OK, we're gonna lay down some heavy stuff.' And he just hung the one mike in there and everybody just sat around and played. It was really primitive but Shadow Morton got incredible sounds out of this crazy little junky studio. The singers used to come in later and lay down the tracks so you never really knew what you were playing on, but there's a piano note on 'Remember (Walking In The Sand)' every once in a while and I *think* that's me."

Billy also believes that he played the dramatic piano chords on The Shangri-Las' later hit 'Leader Of The Pack', but he's not absolutely sure about that either and Shadow Morton certainly doesn't remember – even if he knew at the time. Noted for his absent-mindedness, George Morton was nicknamed "Shadow" by songwriters Jeff Barry and Ellie Greenwich because he never seemed to be around when he was needed but was always hovering there when he wasn't.

Early in 1965, The Detergents had a hit with 'Leader Of The Laundromat', a comical parody of 'Leader Of The Pack'. On the record a voice is heard to ask: "Who's that banging on the piano?" A good question. But one thing is for sure – Billy Joel never got paid for those sessions.

His next major stab at session work proved to be rather more lucrative. In 1967, he was hired to play the organ on a TV ad for Bachman Pretzels. The thrilling vocal line – "There's a new twist in Bachman" – was supplied by Twist legend Chubby Checker and Billy got to do a snatch of Bach at the end. Bach. Bachman. Get it? Joel was paid 200 dollars and met Chubby Checker in

person; he visited Checker's house and saw the great man's "weird-looking" double gold record for 'The Twist' (which went to Number 1 in the US on two separate occasions).

Meanwhile the New York music and club scene had been growing ever more vibrant and active. Along Bleeker and MacDougal Streets, in the Village, the folk traditionalists continued to play in the coffee-house atmosphere of such dives as the Gaslight, the Cafe Wha, the Cafe-Au-Go-Go and the Bitter End, while elsewhere electric house bands like Jordan Christopher and the Wild Ones and Dow Jones and the Industrials were on show in the consciously "swinging" night spots – Arthur, Trude Heller's, Cheetah. Then, during The Beatles Shea Stadium concert in August 1965, a message flashed up on the scoreboard – "The Rascals Are Here".

And very soon they were. The Young Rascals from New Jersey with their blue-eyed soul and organ-dominated sound were to touch off another mini-explosion of New York band activity; by 1967, there were groups playing the new so-called East Coast Sound all over the place, from Scott Muni's Rolling Stone discotheque on East 48th to Ungano's on West 70th to the Cheetah on Broadway. And the centre of activity was a large club outside the city in Island Park called the Action House. Here Long Island groups like

After playing some sleazy hall to three people the night before, he'd slope in late for classes. ". . . I would show up and get a B on the tests but the teachers wouldn't pass me because I wasn't in school enough."

The Vagrants (featuring portly guitarist Leslie West), The Rich Kids, The Illusion, Vanilla Fudge and The Hassles – with one Billy Joel at the Hammond organ – played to the devoted. The corporate sound was a sort of soul-based baroque featuring heavily-vibratoed vocals and melodramatic arrangements,

The Teenie Hassles with their manager Irwin Mazur

a blend of rhythmic funk and "progressive" bombast that was sometimes spot on and other times way over the top.

It was the "East Coast Sound"; it was the "Long Island Sound" and Billy Joel described it thus: "I saw The Young Rascals one night in a little funky dive, a place called the Scene on West 48th Street. It was a real trashy place with fungus on the walls, a lousy place. But The Rascals were great – the best live show I'd ever seen. Their 'blue-eyed' soul was the hottest thing and the other big band at the time were The Vagrants. To this day I still think The Vagrants were the best. And then Vanilla Fudge came out and made a record that was kinda like The Vagrants and that kinda blew apart the whole scene. The Hassles were part of that whole Long Island band scene."

It had soon become obvious to Billy Joel that The Echoes were hurtling towards oblivion. They were pretty big cheeses on the Hicksville church dance circuit, but they never seemed likely to rise above that level. Joel was carrying the band on his talent alone – and that was not enough. His schoolwork was suffering: after playing some sleazy hall to three people the night before, he'd slope in late for classes. "My eyes were red. Teachers thought I was a drug addict. . .I would show up and get a B on the tests but the teachers wouldn't pass me because I wasn't in school enough." He made it to the 12th grade but then was prevented from graduating because of his poor attendance record. Rosalind was upset as she wanted her son to go to college. "Well, if I'm not going to Columbia University, then I'm going to Columbia Records," he assured his mother and promised he'd buy her a house one day. He did.

The Echoes changed their name to The Emerald Lords who in turn became The Lost Souls. This last incarnation of the band was actually offered, tentatively, a short-term recording contract with Mercury records. They recorded demo versions of Billy's songs 'Journey's End' and 'Just Another Lie' but the deal came to nothing. Then, one night in 1967, The Lost Souls found themselves playing a Long Island club on the same bill as The Hassles, one of Long Island's major pop attractions. John Dizek, The Hassles' singer, approached Joel and asked him to join the band. Billy said he would, but only if Lost Souls bassist Howard Blauvelt could join as well. Dizek agreed and went off to sack The Hassles' existing bass player.

The Hassles' R&B and soul-based inclinations re-fired Billy Joel's musical imagination. He began writing once more and scoured record stores for likely, obscure material to cover: "There was this old bus depot record store out of New York where you could buy every 45 in the world. It was called Soul Records and we found all these obscure Sam and Dave things to do." Joel's new optimism was rewarded in mid-1967 when The Hassles were signed to United Artists in New York. Almost immediately, the group – Joel, Blauvelt, Dizek, guitarist Richard McKenner and drummer Jon Small – were put into the studio to record an album under producers Tony Michaels and Vinny Gorman. A funky, "work-out" version of an old Sam and Dave number, 'You Got Me Hummin', was soon issued as a single. (Astonishing fact: Dave Prater of Sam and Dave shares the same birthday as Billy Joel!) It died a rapid death and a follow-up, 'Every Step I Take (Every Move I Make)', credited to T.Michaels/V.Gorman/W.Joel, was released at the end of the year – and when Billy saw the writer's credit, he realised he'd been diddled: "What happened was that the two producers decided they'd get in on some of the royalties. I had actually written the song and they came in and said 'Well, why don't you change a word here and a word there?' and I said OK. I figured these big record company guys knew what they were talking about. I was young and naive so I changed the words. And then they split the writing credit three ways so I'd get one third. But it wasn't a hit anyway, so it didn't make any difference. Ha ha!"

Still, he had at least got his name on a single and, in November, his name appeared on an album sleeve for the first time. Well, a version of his name anyway. "William Joseph Martin Joel, 18. Affectionately known as Billy Joe," read the credit on *The Hassles* LP – "I don't know where the Joseph came from," said Billy. "And it wasn't 'affectionately', it was 'mistakenly'. Nobody could get the 'el' in Joel straight, so I dropped it."

The Hassles fared no better than the group's two singles; their growing band of

Long Island fans might all have rushed out to buy the record, but nobody else did. So, it wasn't the most exciting LP in living memory; nonetheless it did have its moments – a choppy version of 'Fever' with rasping, strangulated vocals from Dizek, a mildly trippy rendition of Traffic's 'Coloured Rain' (Billy was big on Traffic and Stevie Winwood: "If there was one favourite group I ever had it was Traffic. No, it was The Beatles. But if there was one other favourite group it was Traffic. Stevie Winwood had this incredible rhythm and blues screaming voice coming out of this little skinny English kid"), and Gladys Knight and the Pips' minor hit from 1964 'Giving Up', done slow and sloppy with dramatic stops and starts à la Vanilla Fudge. Otherwise the LP was a mish-mash of too many styles coated with a dreadfully stodgy production – Joel's over-derivative originals were particularly weak. 'Every Step I Take (Every Move I Make)' was a Zombies-styled "atmospheric" plodder, 'I Can Tell' was Billy's attempt at turning the band into The Spencer Davis Group and 'Warming Up' was just a lazy filler, a loose instrumental jam with much squealing guitar.

The Hassles themselves detested the album; it was "bubblegum", it was spineless pop fodder, it was weedy and pointless. The group would improve, wouldn't it?

DISCOGRAPHY

THE HASSLES (United Artists; 1967)

SIDE ONE
Warming Up (W.Joel)
Just Holding On (L.Weiss)
A Taste Of Honey (R.Marlow/B.Scott)
Every Step I Take (Every Move I Make)
(W.Michaels/V.Gormann/W.Joel)
Coloured Rain (S.Winwood/J.Capaldi/
C.Wood)

SIDE TWO
I Hear Voices (G.Stashuk)
I Can Tell (W.Joel)
Giving Up (V.McCoy)
Fever (J.Davenport/E.Cooley)
You've Got Me Hummin' (I.Hayes/
D.Porter)

PRODUCER: Tony Michaels & Vinny Gormann
MUSICIANS: Billy Joel *(keyboards);* John Dizek *(vocals);* Howard Blauvelt *(bass);* Richard McKenna *(guitar);* Jon Small *(drums).*

SINGLES:
'You've Got Me Hummin' '; 'Every Step I Take (Every Move I Make)'.

3

THE COSMIC RATIONALE: SHED TEENIE FOR HIP

The Hassles put their debut album behind them, writing it off as an embarrassment, a naive "teenybop" effort. It was time, they decided, to reassess their creative strategy and "get their heads together." All across the nation, throughout 1967, there had been this new vibration of "lurve", peace and LSD, and out on the West Coast countless new bands had been "expressing themselves" through extended acid freak-out symphonies. Looking back from a safe distance, the hippie gumbo muck and cosmic rock of the late Sixties seems charming at best, mindless and grotesque at worst. But at the time it was the *cool* music.

In 1968, Vanilla Fudge – leading lights of the Long Island sound – put out *The Beat Goes On,* produced by Shadow Morton(!), and they set new standards of pretentiousness and absurdity for their contemporaries to follow or ignore as they saw fit. "This album is people throughout the world, their ideas, beliefs, their emotions" droned a laid-back voice seeping sincerity on the Fudge's epic: "We hold only the tools through which to express time through music." The band then proceeded to unleash their terrible and baff-

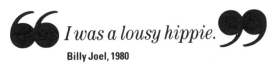

Look! You are encircled by a pentagram of orange leaping flames. Shapes! Are drawing closer and their chanting tongues scream out a thousand names.

'Hour of the Wolf', words and music by Billy Joel and John Dizek, 1969

I was a lousy hippie.

Billy Joel, 1980

ling "concept" in which the entire history of music, politics, philosophy and sociology was set to a doom-laden recurring organ theme and a million babbling sitars. How could The Hassles ignore such a challenge? Unless they at least made a *nod* in the direction of progressive "exploration", the band might well end up the un-hippest thing on Long Island. With a new set of what Billy Joel would later describe – quite accurately – as "stretched out, really preposterous arrangements," The Hassles entered the studio once more.

This time United Artists assigned the group to a more sympathetic producer, Thomas Kaye (who would subsequently work with Steely Dan, Gene Clark and others). Kaye, an eccentric perfectionist, was also looking for something grandiose and "important" from the band and, to this end, he practically imprisoned them in the studio while they worked away on the album project. Joel: "We stayed in this studio, Studio 3, on 48th Street and we were locked in with this maniac producer Tommy Kaye. We actually lived in the studio for six months and it was pitch black so we didn't know if it was big or not and they just used to send food in to us and every once in a while we'd go outside to see what season it was. We got nuts. It was like a bunch of kids running around. You could play any instrument you wanted, use any tape machine, and we ran up this ridiculous budget on this ridiculous album and we went nutty. 'Hey, man! Let's be psychedelic. Oh *wow*!' It was an exercise in self-indulgence – and we weren't even *stoned*."

In *Billboard*, there appeared a headline: "Hassles Come Of Age, Shed Teenie For Hip".

With its self-consciously psychedelic sleeve design, its dippily impressionistic lyrics – concerning colours, flashing silhouettes, summers of meaninglessness, ships of dreams, etc – and its stylised arrangements, which would switch from bombastic to precious without warning, *Hour Of The Wolf* serves as a fine example of the musical excesses of the period. The title track, a 12-minute mini-opera, managed to pack in every acid-rock trick known to man – stoned gibbering over gloomy church organ dirges, extended free-form guitar extemporisations, symphonic intermissions, blustering drum solos, mental exhaustion, etc. Grim and self-important as it was, however, the LP's music was executed with a certain aplomb: the whole thing had a gustily confident swagger about it, as if The Hassles were *defying* the listener to cry "Excuse me but this is crap." And, in general, listeners *didn't*; although *Hour Of The Wolf* was far from being a scorching hit, it sold better than its predecessor and received some remarkably warm reviews. In *Billboard*, dated 17 May 1969, there appeared a headline: "Hassles Come Of Age, Shed Teenie For Hip". Below was a glowing report of a Hassles appearance at Steve Paul's Scene club: "...a shouted comment from a front table told the story. 'You've come a long way, man!'...Gone was the teenie-bopper image that characterized the Long Island act's earlier appearances. Instead, The Hassles were a together, underground group that, in its finest moments, had traces of Procul Harum, and that's quite a

The Hassles

20

The Hassles in a late publicity shot

unit to be compared with." The writer went on to suggest that 'Revenge Is Sweet', the opening number of the set, might be an appropriate title for The Hassles' next album. But there wasn't to be a next album. Shortly after the Scene gigs, Billy Joel and Jon Small quit the band.

He and drummer Jon Small would form a power duo – organ and drums – and "destroy the world with amplification."

Joel was fed up with McKenner's out-of-tune feedback antics. Most undisciplined. And he still felt that the band had a "bubblegum crazy connotation" that he wanted to get well away from. Anyway, he'd had this brainwave. He and drummer Jon Small would form a power duo – organ and drums – and "destroy the world with amplification." Joel had heard Led Zeppelin's first album and had been "totally knocked *out!*" He wanted to make that kind of noise, that beefy, crunching hard rock. It hadn't been called heavy metal yet, but Billy Joel wanted to go heavy metal.

"It was a great idea," insists Billy to this day. "It was a very noble experiment – just me and an organ and a left-handed keybase and wah wah pedals and echo machines and about ten huge amplifiers. And Jon Small playing the drums." They called themselves Attila and they moved into Jon Small's parents' wallpaper store where they spent six months in the basement practising and "blasting ourselves with this incredibly loud music." In the meantime, they'd negotiated a deal with Epic and now they were ready to record and perform. They did a couple of gigs – at one date at the Action House, half the audience apparently fled screaming while the other half went ape for the monstrous noise – and things seemed to be going as planned: "Live, it was really powerful and exciting." But in the recording studio it was a different story: "We were in a four-track studio and the engineer was this German guy who hated any kind of rock'n'roll to begin with and he didn't understand a word we were saying and we didn't know what we were doing. The record

was dismal."

Some might say that "dismal" was too mild a word to describe the full horror of *Attila*. Others might argue that the album was, in fact, a misunderstood classic of kitsch. On the front cover, Joel and Small, dressed as a rampaging pair of Hun warriors, and looking suitably embarrassed about it, stood amidst a load of sides of beef dangling from meat hooks. On the back cover, absurd sleeve notes introduced us to the hot combo: "In the fifth century, a scourge rolled across Eastern Europe, destroying all that stood in its path. A screaming invincible wave of destruction, it left in its wake half the civilized world in shock and bleeding submission. It was a sword and a flame. It was a name that became synonymous with an unstemmable tide of conquest. ATTILA!...ATTILA is the most remarkable group on the scene since the Huns sacked Europe..." And so it went on (and on).

We were told Billy Joel's star sign (Taurus); we were told that he "only sweats two things: perfecting his sound and South East Asia" (whatever that was supposed to mean); we were told that amongst the record's most "crushing, bruising" numbers were such pearls as 'Amplifier Fire', 'Godzilla', 'March Of The Huns' and 'Brain Invasion' – "a kind of stereo look at the insides of minds and things." After that kind of introduction, the LP's music had a lot to live up to – but it managed it. It was *horrible*. Joel wailed and squealed in grim and ghastly mimicry of Robert Plant while his Hammond organ, model #3, thundered and chundered and roared and whined and Small battered and splattered and thrashed away at his drums. So much effort! What a racket! Sound and fury signifying nothing very much at all.

Before the album had even been released, however, Attila was a dead duck. Late in 1969 an LP titled *Lee Michaels* began to move up the US album charts – Lee Michaels played the organ while a guy named Bartholomew Smith Frost, Frosty for short, hit the drums. Meanwhile, in Britain, keyboard player Eddie Hardin and drummer Pete York, ex-member of The Spencer Davis Group, had teamed up as Hardin & York and were billing themselves as "The World's Smallest Big Band". Joel's novel power duo concept no longer seemed so novel after all. "And that," according to Billy, "was the end of Attila. Thank God. A timely death."

Attila's break-up left Billy understandably depressed – he has described this post-Attila period as one of "great self-pity." But disappointment at the band's failure was only one of many problems that he faced at the end of 1970; he had broken up with a girlfriend with whom he had a very serious relationship and, most immediately, he was out of money. Billy has claimed that he was so broke he couldn't pay any rent, sometimes sleeping in all-night laundromats; in sub-freezing New York winters they were the warmest places to sleep. He didn't want to go back to his mother's house in Hicksville because, down and out as you can get, you sure don't want your family to know about it. But, in desperation, he did return to mother. Where he made a – possibly half-hearted – attempt at suicide.

"I went into the closet and said, 'I'm gonna kill myself.' There were two things inside. There was chlorine bleach and I said, 'Nah, that's gonna taste bad.' So I took the Pledge. And all I ended up doing was farting furniture polish."

According to an interview Billy gave to Chris Connelly of *Rolling Stone* in 1982: "I think that when you're that age, you're really hung up on yourself. You take yourself too damn seriously. . . I went through a depression where I just felt suicidal. I even tried to do myself in. I went into the closet and said, 'I'm gonna kill myself.' There were two things inside. There was chlorine bleach and I said, 'Nah, that's gonna taste bad.' So I took the Pledge. And all I ended up doing was farting furniture polish. I'd sit on my mother's chair and polish the furniture. . . That's when I said this is really sick." Furniture polish. Hardly the final solution – more of a "cry for help". In the end, Billy ended up checking himself into Meadowbrook Hospital where he was placed under immediate psychiatric observation.

Short as it was, the stint there had a big impact on him. As he put it: "Other people have religion or scientology or shrinks or whatever. Me, I had the nuthouse." For Billy, it was a nightmare right out of *One Flew Over The Cuckoo's Nest.* "They give you a smock to wear with your ass hanging out," he reminisced in *Playboy,* "and they give you Thorazine all the time. You can't carry matches, razor blades, no personal possessions, and you sleep in a big room with all those other guys. They keep you sedated all the time while they observe you. I'd walk over to the nurse's station and knock on the window and go, 'Hey, I'm OK. These other people are crazy. So can I get out of here?' And they'd go, 'Sure Mr Joel. Here's your Thorazine,' and they would close the gate. I'd just watch the other people who were really crazy." These crazy people included heroin addicts, rapists, alcoholics, irretrievable schizophrenics, and a man who thought he was Kaiser Wilhelm; but it was their example that shocked Billy out of his self-pity and self-indulgence. He convinced the doctors that he was indeed OK and walked out of Meadowbrook: "I got out and the door closed behind me and I walked down the street and said, 'Oh, I'll never get that low again.' It was one of the best things I ever did, because I've never gotten to feel sorry for myself, no matter what's happened. Any kind of problem since then is nothing compared with what I've seen other people go through."

Billy Joel had been through a belated sort of adolescence – a crack-up of a minor kind – and, thankfully, he'd pulled himself together before things could get out of hand. While his friends were marching off to Vietnam, he'd been wallowing in a mire of "angst" and juvenile self-pity. As he later confessed: "There's just a time when you feel so isolated and sorry for yourself and almost nobody can help you. Even if you have somebody, there comes a time when you feel totally alone. That's the worst thing you can do, feel so sorry for yourself that you can't think straight anymore." This experience was to prove a tonic and, when he got out, he told himself, "I can make music and I can fall in love again."

But although Billy knew he could make music again, the desire for personal fame had gone. The failure of The Hassles and Attila had convinced him that his talents lay in songwriting, not performing on stage and singing his own material. "Enough of this rock and roll stardom," Billy told himself, "I had gotten the ego thing out of my system." He wanted to write songs for other people to perform. This was a curious sort of retrograde thinking.

Since The Beatles, most, if not all, popular groups – especially the ones Billy admired – wrote their own material. In fact, it was a show of rebellion to do it. Before The Beatles, most artists didn't write much of their own material; with few exceptions, top artists were dependent on producers, managers, and record companies to provide material for them, keeping them in an artistic stranglehold. Part of the reason the Sixties were such an explosive time, musically speaking, was that artists wrested control from the businessmen to choose and write their own material without regard for incestuous publishing deals and third-party personal favours. And soon, all those little rooms in places like the Brill Building, where writing teams had been pounding out hits for a fee and recording hopeful demos, were quiet and empty. Some of those writers, like Carole King, Neil Sedaka and Neil Diamond, went on to performing careers, others just quietly faded away.

The failure of The Hassles and Attila had convinced him that his talents lay in songwriting.

The cult of singer/songwriter was reaching its peak just at the time when Billy was deciding to become a quiet, behind-the-scenes man. In early 1971, a *Time* cover story heralded the arrival of "soft rock", an exciting new genre which basically meant a man or woman alone with a guitar, piano and a song. The biggest star in this glittering firmament was James Taylor, whose 1970 LP, *Sweet Baby James,* made him one of the biggest record sellers, concert draws and role models in American popular music. From virtually every dorm room in the country came the melancholy ballads of the early Elton John, Cat Stevens, Joni Mitchell, Carole King

(whose *Tapestry* is one of the biggest-selling LPs of all time) and Jackson Browne – all of whom had their own "meaningful" experiences to write about and would not be spending their time listening to demos from nobodies from Long Island.

So it seems almost wilfully perverse that Billy should decide to become a songwriter at this time. Who did he think was going to record his songs, David Cassidy? But nonetheless, he went about putting together a demo of his songs.

In 1971, Billy was signed to Family Productions, a Los Angeles label owned by veteran producer and wheeler-dealer Artie Ripp. According to Billy, he wound up signed to Family as part of a deal that Michael Lang (one of the organizers of Woodstock) made with Ripp. Billy had sent a tape of his demos to Lang's Sunshine Records, a small, upstate New York company, and later signed with them. Billy then got transferred to Family with other Sunshine artists. In another version of the story reported in *Crawdaddy,* Lang was visiting Artie Ripp in California and played the tape for Ripp who, thrilled by what he heard, got in touch with Billy immediately. Following the advice of his then-manager, Irwin Mazur, who had also been The Hassles' manager, Billy signed to Family Productions to record his first LP. Whichever way it happened, it was a move that would have disastrous consequences.

Billy moved out to California to record the LP – to be titled *Cold Spring Harbor* – and the whole thing, from beginning to end, was a nightmare. As Billy recalled, "It wasn't supposed to be this heavily produced, legendary thing. They were very simple songs and Artie Ripp got a hold of it. It took a year to record, which was insane. It should have taken three weeks. It was going to be a demonstration album of songs. But once you sing a song five or six times in the studio, you start to lose any kind of spontaneity or feeling for it. Artie's style of recording is two hundred times. 'Let's just do it one more time.' 'Artie, I've done it two hundred times.' 'We can still get the perfect one.' At that point I was like a robot. I didn't even care anymore."

Even if the LP was just supposed to be a vehicle for other performers to hear his songs, there was an absurd blunder that made even that modest goal impossible. In the mastering process, the tapes were speeded up and Billy's voice sounded "like a chipmunk." After the year that it took to record that "meisterwork", Ripp convinced Billy that he had to go out and tour in support of the LP, a move that turned out to be another fiasco. After hastily assembling a band, Billy went out on tour for six months after which he wound up broke and disgusted. He was never paid for the tour; he and the band got mostly "cigarette money. . . sometimes we'd get meals taken care of, but mostly we paid for our own food. After six months we were going 'Hey, what's going on? Aren't we gonna get paid any money?' I was told, 'Oh, it's all promotion.' And I found out there was a lot of money that went by." To make matters worse, during this big promotional tour Billy never even saw the record for sale in a store or heard any of its tracks played on the radio.

For his part, Artie Ripp has maintained a low profile in recent years. In *Crawdaddy*, he told his side of the story to Timothy White, insisting that he never intended to do Billy in, but was caught in a bind. He insists that a little bit into the recording process he realized that "what I bought myself was the world's first platinum coffin with diamond studs – meaning that no matter how good my records were, Gulf and Western's Paramount Records (the company that Ripp had a deal with to distribute Family Production's records) would never be a successful record company. . .Billy and Irwin and I were making a great record that's gonna die."

Cold Spring Harbor, technical problems aside, is not a great record. 'She's Got A Way' is about the most successful song on an LP full of Beatle influences and even that is reminiscent of more syrupy Beatle compositions – the 'Something' comparison is inevitable, and on 'You Can Make Me Free' Billy even sings he can "wait a lonely lifetime," a phrase that's got the McCartney patent. This first album seems very much tailored for artists other than himself – certainly Billy was hoping that other people would buy the songs. The lush, heavy strings and ponderous piano capture the dirge-like sound of early Seventies soft rock and the lyrics are post-hippie odes to birds, artists, songs and warm earth mothers, a "mind-set" that Billy never

felt very comfortable with in the first place. Only 'Everybody Loves You Now', the most upbeat track on the record with its rolling piano, and mention of the Staten Island Ferry, provides any hint of Billy's future, more cynical and tougher, work. Although the re-released version of the LP has corrected the problems with the mastering, Billy's voice is all over the place, at times a Tim Buckley falsetto and, at other times, particularly 'Tomorrow Is Today', a weird, unrecognizable, country bass. Billy has kept 'She's Got A Way' and 'Everybody Loves You Now' in his repertoire (they appear on *Songs In The Attic)*, but has wisely left the rest far behind.

Artie Ripp was very cavalier about the recording, which must have disturbed Billy. "None of us were aware of it, OK?" he said. "Nor did we want to pay attention to it. So the musical back-up sucks, the mixes suck and the fidelity on the records sucks. I said to Billy, 'It doesn't matter if it's fast, it doesn't matter if it's slow. Paramount ain't gonna bring this record home.' " And if that weren't enough to make Billy a little insecure, listen to Artie on the subject of the subsequent tour: "I know they're not the world's greatest," Ripp admits he told Billy about the band he was going out on the road with, "but they're the best we can afford." And, as for the lack of payment, Artie doesn't even mind acknowledging that the band didn't get paid often: "Maybe he didn't get money and the band didn't get money, but neither was he sold to some Communist organization . . . Life is not perfect." In his defence, Ripp says that he invested a substantial sum of his own money, at least a couple of hundred thousand dollars, in Billy and "never made him sign no piece of paper other than the original contract."

He didn't have to, because in addition to signing a recording deal, Billy also signed all his publishing over to Family, as well as "all my copyrights and most of my royalties. It was a real screw job." He has said, when asked why he wound up in such a pitiful state of affairs, "What the hell did I know? I was twenty-one which is old enough to be legal and sign things away, but still young enough to be stupid."

After the six month *Cold Spring Harbor* tour, Billy went home to the house he was living in by the ocean in the Hamptons (the

Elizabeth Weber Joel and Billy

working-class section, not the wealthy playground area). He was more or less paid an allowance by his record company; then, one month, a rent check failed to materialize and Billy decided to take drastic measures. "I hate being in debt," he noted. "I hate owing money. That was it. I said: 'To hell with this. I'm going to get out of this field one way or another.' " Billy decided to move to Los Angeles: his lawyer was there, as was Family Productions. "I figured that they weren't going to look for me right under their noses."

Billy wasn't alone on this dramatic trek across the country. The station-wagon carrying his belongings was Elizabeth Weber's, Jon Small's ex-wife and Billy's girlfriend. With them came Elizabeth's son Jason, who was also living with the couple.

Elizabeth and Billy had met in Long Island in the mid-Sixties when she was Jon's girlfriend. According to Billy, they had been friends since The Hassles era, but didn't meet up again until after Billy had finished making *Cold Spring Harbor*. While Billy was in California, Elizabeth and Jon had divorced and Billy began seeing a lot of her when he came back to Oyster Bay. The couple eventually moved into the house in Hampton Bays together. When they first re-met, Elizabeth was attending Adelphi College in Garden City, but dropped out to be with Billy during the terrible tour.

After their marriage in 1973, she enrolled at UCLA's Graduate School of Management, because, as she told *Forbes*, "When we started to live together, I wasn't even sure if Billy was talented. I thought I might have to support him. I was in love." Although she didn't get her degree from UCLA, she learned enough about the byzantine intricacies of business to help Billy solve his problems with Family, renegotiate his subsequent contract with Columbia Records and eventually manage her husband.

Many unpleasant things have been said and insinuated about Elizabeth Joel's management relationship with Billy, the implication being that she was some sort of svengaliette who ruthlessly pushed her affable spouse to superstardom, gleefully counting up the money all the while. Billy defended his wife in *Playboy* by noting that a lot of her reputation was the result of male hostility to strong,

"If you can't trust your wife to manage you, who can you trust?"

professional women. "That image comes from the fact that she's a good business person. She's very soft and gentle, but when she's protecting her business interests, she can be as tough as the next guy." He also suggested that Elizabeth was the model for most of his songs about women. In spite of his one-of-the-guys image, Billy has written more sympathetically and humanely than a lot of other composers, and the women in his songs have run the whole gamut of human types from hippie angel to confused girl to wise and sadder older woman to raging bitch. When asked if Elizabeth was the model for these portraits, Billy responded, "Yes. Sometimes it's specific and sometimes she represents women to me. I use her as a model like painters use their wives and mistresses. She represents all women." Now, that's hardly the talk of a man imprisoned by his wife's ambition.

Billy was very happy for Elizabeth to run his career, affectionately referring to her as the family capitalist and to himself as the more easygoing socialist, happy with his motorcycles, house and credit cards. And the indications are, at least in the beginning, that Elizabeth's business acumen was a very good thing for their marriage. "I kinda expect her to be good at what she does," Billy said at the time. "She can't do what I do. It keeps us interested in each other."

DISCOGRAPHY

HOUR OF THE WOLF
(United Artists; 1969)

SIDE ONE
Country Boy (W. Joel/J. Small)
Night After Day (W. Joel)
Hour Of The Wolf (W. Joel/J. Dizek)
4 O'Clock In The Mornin' (W. Joel)

SIDE TWO
Cat (W. Joel)
Hotel St George (W. Joel)
Land Of Despair (W. Joel/J. Small)
Further Than Heaven (W. Joel/J. Dizek)

PRODUCER: Thomas Kaye
MUSICIANS: Billy Joel *(keyboards, vocals);* Howard Blauvelt *(bass);* Richard McKenner *(guitar);* Jon Small *(drums).*

ATTILA (Epic; 1970)

SIDE ONE
Wonder Woman
California Flash
Revenge Is Sweet
Amplifier Fire
Part I – **Godzilla**
Part II – **March Of The Huns**

SIDE TWO
Rollin' Home
Tear This Castle Down
Holy Moses
Brain Invasion

ALL WORDS AND MUSIC: William Joel & Jonathan Small
PRODUCER: Irwin Mazur, William Joel and Jonathan Small
MUSICIANS: Billy Joel *(keyboards, vocals);* Jon Small *(drums).*

COLD SPRING HARBOR
(Family; 1972)

SIDE ONE
She's Got A Way
You Can Make Me Free
Everybody Loves You Now
Why Judy Why
Falling Of The Rain

SIDE TWO
Turn Around
You Look So Good To Me
Tomorrow Is Today
Nocturne
Got To Begin Again

ALL WORDS AND MUSIC: Billy Joel
PRODUCER: Artie Ripp
MUSICIANS: Rhys Clark, Denny Siewell, Mike McGee *(drums);* Don Evans, Sal De Troia, *(guitar);* Joe Osborn, Larry Knechtel *(bass);* Sneaky Pete Kleinow *(pedal steel guitar);* Al Campbell, L. D. Dixon *(additional keyboards).*

SINGLES:
'She's Got A Way';
'Tomorrow Is Today'.

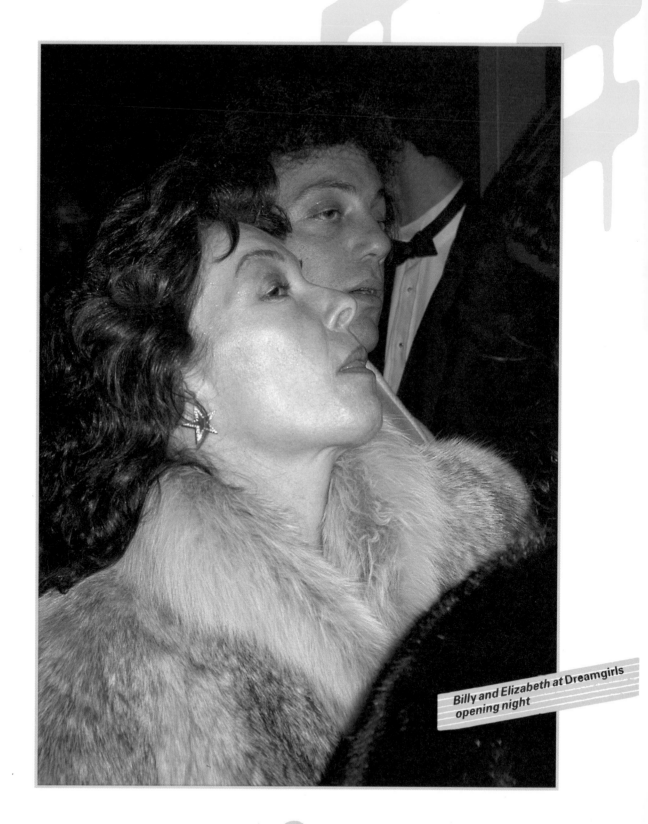

Billy and Elizabeth at Dreamgirls opening night

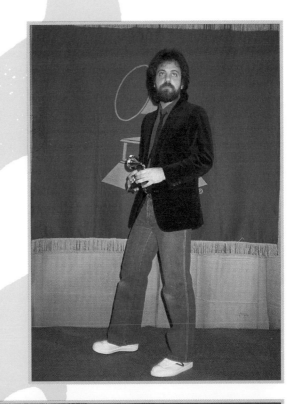

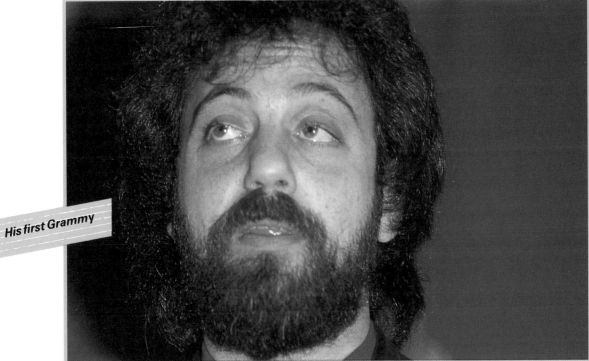

His first Grammy

4

THESE BARS HAVE MADE A PRISONER OUT OF ME

Down in Los Angeles, hiding out and killing time, Billy Joel went looking for work. His intention was to play the piano in some bar. What could be more apt? Playing piano was the only job he really knew. And bar-rooms were his natural habitat. Billy was never into hanging out with the beautiful people, he was a neighbourhood bar person, a Scotch and cigarettes man to the ground. He soon got a gig at a dive called Corky's where, to maintain secrecy, he worked under the name Bill Martin.

After just two weeks tickling Corky's ivories, the new piano man got canned. It was coming up to Christmas and the management wanted a girl singer, someone with "a big body, y'know," to entertain the clientele over the festive season. Bill Martin's replacement "couldn't play worth a damn but she was better looking than I was."

It didn't take him long to find another position; a bar in LA's Wilshire district, the Executive Lounge, took him on and they even put up a little sign in the window, "Billy Martin At The Keyboards". It was a gruelling routine, five hours, 9pm to 2am, each night, doing requests for fearful tear-jerking ballads like 'Feelings' or, even worse, 'Jeremiah Was A Bullfrog (Joy To The World)'. "I didn't know most of the requests I got. Somebody would say 'Play "Here's That Rainy Day" ' and I'd think, 'Uh oh, I don't know that song.' "

But he quickly learned to fake his way through – "Just play a lot of major seventh

> **"** *Sometimes I feel like I should fly on to the stage with a big cape and a big 'P' on my chest – It's a bird! It's a plane! It's Piano Man!* **"**
>
> **Billy Joel, 1977**

chords in a stock kind of progression and you can play any standard in the world." Picking up tips was a cinch too. If there was a guy in the bar who looked Italian, Billy would play the *Godfather* theme; if there was someone who looked Irish, it'd be 'Danny Boy'. With regular five dollar bill gratuities stuffed into the brandy glass, plus union-scale rates of pay, plus Elizabeth's wages – the Executive Lounge had hired her as a cocktail waitress – the couple were doing OK. But being a piano man in a cocktail lounge did have its dangers. Billy began to feel that he'd end up an incurable cynic or die from alcohol poisoning or both. He was in an "alcoholic daze" most of the time sitting there with his shirt unbuttoned and his collar turned up like Buddy Greco. Sometimes he thought he *was* Buddy Greco and he didn't like it. Angelique and Russell Norton, who owned the Executive Lounge, were more than satisfied with Bill Martin's work – he was reliable, he was a good player and he was even picking up a following. Angelique couldn't help noticing that he *definitely* didn't like it when people started singing along. However, one night he managed to defuse an ugly situation with a sing-along for which Angelique was most grateful. A Japanese man had come into the bar and, seeing the Lounge's red decor, started ranting about Reds and Commies and waving a gun about. Billy struck up the tune of 'God Bless America' and everyone in the joint started to sing.

This distracted the Japanese gentleman long enough for someone to grab and disarm him. Hurrah!

Billy Joel stuck it out at the Executive Lounge for six months. Almost every night someone would come up and say: "Hey kid. You could do real good in the music business."

If there was a guy in the bar who looked Italian, Billy would play the *Godfather* theme; if there was someone who looked Irish, it'd be 'Danny Boy'.

The piano player would reply: "Nyah, nah. It's a dirty racket. I just want to sit here and play Hoagy Carmichael tunes and Frank Sinatra songs." And all the time he was sitting there thinking: "I'm gonna get a song out of this. I'm *gonna* get a song out of this." The song he got was 'Piano Man' and it was released as a single on Columbia Records on 23 October 1973.

Columbia had been interested in Billy Joel since seeing him at the Mar Y Sol Festival and hearing him at a Philadelphia concert broadcast live on WMMR-FM in 1972 (a tape of the song 'Captain Jack' would be played on the radio station for months afterwards). Eventually, Columbia tracked the singer down on the West Coast and company boss Clive Davis paid him a visit at the Executive Lounge. The deal was negotiated with Artie Ripp (Ripp would still keep a tidy chunk of the action and the Family Productions "Romulus and Remus" logo would continue to appear on Joel's records) and Billy Joel signed to the new label.

Whilst working the piano bar, Joel had spent his days writing songs in the house he and Elizabeth rented in the mountains above Malibu and he had more than enough for an album. So Columbia put him straight in the studio with producer Michael Stewart. The working relationship did not get off to a merry start. Billy wanted to use the guys from his former band on the album but Stewart, who felt more comfortable with

Hollywood session pros, was uncooperative, making it clear that he had little time for amateurs who couldn't even read charts. Frustrated by Stewart's attitude, Joel's boys walked out of the sessions and Stewart got his own way and his own men.

Billy was initially unhappy with the sound of the finished album; he thought that his voice sounded like a mushy powder-puff. But when the 'Piano Man' single began to climb the national charts in the early spring of 1974, he perked up considerably – "I said 'This is a hit song? You gotta be kidding me. It's just the same chorus over and over.'" Nonetheless, people seemed to like it even though many mistook it for a Harry Chapin song. Even Joel himself was forced to agree that the circular structure, the narrative style and the characters picked out from the piano bar – John the bartender, Paul the real-estate broker and would-be novelist, Davy the sailor – sounded a lot like Chapin's style: "Yeah, it was a *story* song and a lot of people thought it was Harry Chapin. And a lot of other people got the idea that I was kinda mellow and folksy – but that was the only song I ever wrote like that."

'Piano Man' reached its highest chart position of Number 25 in April, and airplay of the single helped to introduce the public to the *Piano Man* album – sales were slow, but they were steady and the LP would be certified gold (500,000 units sold) by the Record Industry Association of America in 1975, two years after its release. American critics, however, were less than enthusiastic about *Piano Man;* by the mid-Seventies, the introspective singer-songwriter had become something of a cliché. "Sensitive", reserved figures who shunned glamour and whose potential appeal lay in their melancholy self-absorption were all over the place. Leonard Cohen, Joni Mitchell, James Taylor, Gordon Lightfoot, Carole King, Laura Nyro, Melanie, Jackson Browne, J.D.Souther, Jesse Winchester, Rick Roberts, assorted members of Crosby Stills Nash and Young on solo trips – was it any wonder the average rock critic was getting a bit sick of all the stern faces and the gentle tunes? When Billy Joel finally appeared, rather late in the day, popping up with *Piano Man,* he was taken for just one more miserable minstrel searching his soul in song.

In Britain, however, where it was the trend for brash, flashy glam pop/rock that was testing the patience of the deeply "serious" critics, *Piano Man* received a fairer hearing, and there were a few writers who felt (or conned themselves into feeling) that they detected a major new talent in Billy Joel. His sharp ear for dialogue, his observations of "oppressive urban realities", his use of various forms of American music, suggested to English outsiders, worshipping American dreams from afar, a musician/poet of the street. *Let It Rock,* the critics' magazine, described *Piano Man* as a "superb album [that] displays a mastery of form and content. No one has brought such a variation of styles to a rock format with such effect." Such lavish praise was, in retrospect, just a little bit over the top, for although *Piano Man* was an intriguing work – an album that reflected the bitter and hardening experiences of Joel's recent years – it was by no means flawless.

At his worst, Billy Joel remained over-dependent on the musical styles of his elders: 'Ain't No Crime', for example, was a piece of gospel-type rock that sounded as if it had been lifted directly off a Leon Russell album, while 'You're My Home' and 'Stop In Nevada' were the kind of ballads that were being trotted out by any number of weedy, long-haired troubadors of the West Coast. But when Joel allowed his wit and his cynical edge to cut through, the album began to wake up. 'The Ballad Of Billy The Kid' with its tongue-in-cheek introduction – clippity-clopping horse hooves and mournful, home-on-the-range cowboy harmonica – was an engaging spoof on rock music's new-found "nostalgia" for the old west, typified by The Eagles' *Desperado* album. 'Billy The Kid' pitted the six gun against the six pack, the streets of Dodge City versus the sprawl of suburbia. "When you're growing up in New York," Billy would say, "you hear these names like Whelan, West Virginia, and it sounds real exotic. But I've been there and it *ain't* exotic. And that song is actually a nonsense song. It's an absolute lie, totally historically inaccurate from beginning to end. Billy the Kid wasn't hanged, he was shot. He never got to Colorado. He never got to Oklahoma. He never left New Mexico as a matter of fact. But I always wanted to write a movie soundtrack like *The*

Magnificent Seven. Nobody asked me so I just totally made one up."

This western tale of the absurd apart, *Piano Man*'s most striking number was the closing track 'Captain Jack', a sour look at the dismal life of a poor little rich kid who hangs around in new English clothes, picking

---

When the 'Piano Man' single began to climb the national charts in the early spring of 1974, he perked up considerably – "I said 'This is a hit song? You gotta be kidding me. It's just the same chorus over and over.' "

---

the nose and waiting for somebody – Captain Jack – to come by with some drugs. With lines like "You just sit home and masturbate," the song was pretty strong stuff, but it was funny too: this kid is 21 but mother still makes the bed and they just found father in the swimming-pool. If perhaps a little self-righteous, 'Captain Jack' dealt with the whole bone-headed drug "scoring" process just as effectively as that other song on the subject, Velvet Underground's 'Waiting For The Man': waiting for Captain Jack to turn up with the goods is a mind-numbing way to waste a life – but then every time he *does* show up there's that rousing chorus that seems to make it all worth while. . .for a moment. "At the time, I saw so many good friends of mine being so stupid with one drug or another," says Billy. The song wasn't preaching "Don't take drugs" because "Drugs can be fun. It was more like trying to smack somebody in the face, saying 'Don't do it just because it's hip!' It's a sicko song." Sicko, maybe, but it was the song that had made him a cult star in Philadelphia. Almost everywhere else, however, he remained the guy who'd done that Harry Chapin song.

With his backing band – guitarist Don Evans, bass player Pat McDonald, drummer Rhys Clark and banjo/pedal steel guitar player Tom Whitehorse – Billy made a number of

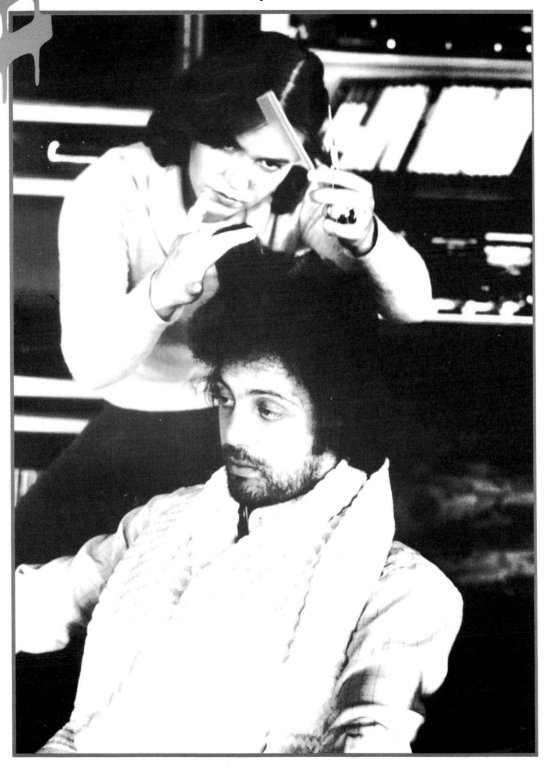

live appearances during 1974. In Philadelphia, he was already big enough to headline at minor concert venues, but on the West Coast he was still a stranger and, opening for acts like The Doobie Brothers, J.Geils Band and The Beach Boys, he often felt unwelcome. "Opening in those huge places was a real tough slot. Nobody wanted to see the opening act, they wanted to see the headliner. You just couldn't go up there and do 'Piano Man' because the crowd wanted to hear 'Help Me Rhonda'. So I would say something outrageous or do my Joe Cocker impersonation – anything to get attention. We'd do 'Jumpin' Jack Flash'. We'd say 'Throw out all the sweet stuff, let's do the barbarian set!' I guess I picked up a certain amount of smarts." But "smarts" are sometimes not enough. . .

DISCOGRAPHY

PIANO MAN (1979)

ONE SIDE
Travellin' Prayer
Piano Man
Ain't No Crime
You're My Home
The Ballad Of Billy The Kid

ANOTHER SIDE
Worse Comes To Worst
Stop In Nevada
If I Only Had The Words (To Tell You)
Somewhere Along The Line
Captain Jack

ALL WORDS AND MUSIC: Billy Joel
PRODUCER: Michael Stewart
MUSICIANS: Larry Carlton/Richard Bennet/Dean Parks *(guitars);* Wilton Felder/Emory Gordy *(bass);* Ron Tutt/Rhys Clark *(drums);* Michael Omartian *(accordian);* Eric Weissberg/Fred Heilbrun *(banjos);* Billy Armstrong *(violin)*

SINGLES:
'Piano Man';
'The Ballad Of Billy The Kid';
'Travellin' Prayer';
'Worse Comes To Worst';
'If I Only Had The Words (To Tell You)'.

5

SLEEPING WITH THE TELEVISION ON

In the summer of 1974, Billy Joel went back into Devonshire Sound studios in North Hollywood and began work on a follow-up to *Piano Man*. The new album was to be produced by Michael Stewart, again, and although Don Evans and Tom Whitehorse were allowed to contribute this time, it was a virtually unchanged cast of professional sessioneers who provided the backing. Released that autumn, *Streetlife Serenade*, rather than building on the limited success of *Piano Man*, proved to be a hesitant and shaky step to nowhere very much at all. The sound was much as before but the scope and imagination of the earlier album were missing. The inclusion of two instrumentals, 'Root Beer Rag' – a rinky-dinky ragtime thing that allowed Joel to show off at the ivories – and 'The Mexican Connection' – a section of ultimately pointless film music – suggested that the artist had run low on ideas; a number like 'Root Beer Rag' was fine in concert, a "crowd-pleaser" as they say, but what was it doing on a studio album? And then there were songs like

> 66 *This next song is dedicated to what I refer to as 'rock'n'roll jive.' OK, let me give you some examples. . .You go to a concert and the first thing the band does when they come on is they automatically demand that you 'put your hands together' – 'Hey! Come on everybody!' . . . One night I'd like to see a group like that come on and go 'Hey now! Let's all clap our hands and boogie and rock'n'roll!' And the whole audience just goes. . .'No' . . . 'Er, hey, they're not doing it man. Maybe we'll have to play some au-then-tic music. . .'* 99

Billy Joel introducing 'The Entertainer' on stage in Philadelphia, 1980

'The Great Suburban Showdown' which sounded far closer to Jackson Browne's vision of suburban ennui than to BJ's own: "You couldn't help but be influenced by Jackson Browne if you lived in California," Billy later admitted. "He was just typical of Southern California sound and he *got* to me." When Jackson Browne starts getting to you, you know you've been in California too long. . .

Once more, it was only when Billy allowed the darker, more jaded side of his nature to sneak through that the album showed any signs of life. And the highpoint of *Streetlife Serenade* was 'The Entertainer', a jaunty and acid musical monologue delivered by a creepy singing star who treats his fans and his record company with equal contempt. The creepy star/narrator knows the fans will forget him once he's off the charts and, to keep him *on* the charts, the company will do unspeakable things to his "art" like taking the most brilliant song he ever wrote and chopping it down to "3.05" – "If you're gonna have a hit, you've got to make it fit." That's showbiz.

Released as a single (unedited), 'The Entertainer' reached Number 34 in the *Billboard* chart in December 1974. Most people took the song for what it was – a gibe at creepy singing stars and the whole rotten business. Some, however – snooty critics of America's increasingly "intellectual" rock press – were convinced that Joel was singing about *himself,* whining unbearably like a tortured artiste. Which would have been some conceit. "A lot of people assume that everything I write is 'me, myself, moi, I, me, I,'" Billy commented. "But, frankly, I'm very boring. 'The Entertainer' is not autobiographical – totally. Some of the verses I'm in and others I'm out."

"Roy Orbison had a lot of trouble with his career because people couldn't stand to look at him on stage, he was so strange looking. He looked like all his joints weren't connected right, so I kinda feel an affinity with him."

In later years, he would give entertaining accounts of how the song had been created: "I was watching one of those TV rock shows like *Midnight Special* or Don Kirschner, one of those shows with assembly-line groups. One group came on with 15-inch platforms, another group came on with little lightning bolts coming off their heads. . .It got so jive that I really got grossed out. I said 'Aw, come *on!*,' picked up a guitar – and I don't even really play guitar – and started writing, sticking a pin in the whole 'Rock Star As God' syndrome." And on stage, years later, he would introduce the song with a perfectly-timed comic rap about rock stars with bloated egos, heavy metal studs with bananas down their trousers, rock'n'roll jive and cheap stunts in the name of "entertainment". Pompous pop and dismal rock had always conspired to get Billy's goat – particularly when they were up on TV.

Even when he first struck it big, Billy Joel hated appearing on TV. He didn't think he looked quite right – he felt a lot like Roy Orbison: "Roy Orbison had a lot of trouble with his career because people couldn't stand to look at him on stage, he was so strange looking. He looked like all his joints weren't connected right, so I kinda feel an affinity with him." He also loathed the way in which music was presented on the small screen: even if you looked all right to begin with, the TV producers would manage to make you end up looking stupid: "TV's idea of rock is like a Las Vegas set-up with dopey silver foil things hanging behind you and dancing girls come out and you might as well be Andy Williams. Network TV people and Hollywood film producer-type people, they all have their own concept of rock'n' roll. They don't understand it. Watch any of those old rock'n'roll movies in the Sixties and there's always a scene where they go in the discotheque and there's some guy who hired a kid and his band to do the music for the discotheque and everybody's doing the frug and it's like 'Wow! This is the *worst* music I've ever *heard!*' I hate those movies. They go to the ski lodge and there's The Astronauts with their white Fender guitars going 'doo-dwap-a-doo-dang.'"

In the Eighties Billy Joel would be forced, by pop's new accent on the promotional video, to stick his face on the TV screen (but no Las Vegas showgirls or dopey silver foil thank you very much, matey). In the Seventies, he avoided TV spots (with notable exceptions – such as his 1977 appearance on *Saturday Night Live*) wherever possible: "I don't *do* TV," he said. "Only by mistake. Or if someone scheisters me." Pop TV was drippy and cheesy and not to be trusted. Imagine Billy Joel's reaction, then, when shortly after 'The Entertainer' had made the charts he was half-watching some half-baked chat'n'pop show and, amid streamers of silver foil, spangly dancing girls, etc, Mr Anthony Newley came on to do a singing spot. "I am the entertainer . . ." he began to warble. Anthony Newley, who had squandered his talent years ago, who was now an archetypal showbiz hack, crooning 'The Entertainer' on some horrible half-witted TV show that probably nobody in the world – apart from the staggered Billy Joel – was actually watching. That seemed to say it all, really.

One morning in 1975, Billy Joel woke up and said "What am I still doing here in California? I'm a New Yorker." It was about time.

He and Elizabeth had been out there on the West Coast for three years now. They'd embraced much of the life-style of California's upwardly-mobile, sun-kissed ex-hippies. They'd gotten "mellow". They'd taken to "natural foods". They'd smoked a little pot now and then. Billy had even done acid, though only once: "I saw rocks move. It scared the hell out of me." And he'd even found himself using "cosmic" figures of speech like "cerebrally environmental, man". This laid-back atmosphere was all very well, but for a suburban New York boy, there was something desperately lacking – a certain edge, a darkish sense of humour. Things were altogether different back East, as Billy has said: "In New York, if you're friends with somebody, you walk up to him and you go 'Hey stooopid!' and he goes 'Hey jerk!' and you smack him. It means 'I love you, man!' But in California if I did that, they'd go like 'Oh wow. You're so *ho-stile!*' " It was time to go home.

The songs for *Streetlife Serenade* had not flowed easily and it showed: "I wrote some horrible songs when I was doing that album. There was one called 'In The Streets'; it was like a Bob Dylan thing – 'but you were so *romantic* when you were in the street. . .' The melody was sticky, the rhythm was lousy and the words were really stupid. But we *recorded* it. I had Michael Stewart erase it – I didn't want anybody to ever hear it." The songs that people *did* hear were, apart from 'The Entertainer', hardly stunning either and the album had flopped. And during the 1975 "Streetlife Serenade" tour, Billy began to realize that he'd have to return to New York to recapture his creative edge. But it was news of New York City's financial crisis that finally spurred him home: "The financial crisis came up and New York was going to go under. It was dying and that was the turning-point that made me go back. New York was going down the tubes and in California there was a lot of smug 'ha ha ha'. So I went back. As a writer, I just had to be there. It was a place for people to go and observe the future of the American city. The financial backruptcy, the supposedly incredible crime rate, all the problems, everything was there that could be the future."

Once back East, he and Elizabeth moved into a house north of New York City in Highland Falls between West Point and Bear Mountain. And within 20 minutes of entering the new house, Billy had composed a song called, appropriately enough, 'New York State Of Mind': "It was like one of those spontaneous 'vomit' things – it just popped out. I envisaged Ray Charles singing it at the opening of the World Series instead of the National Anthem." (Billy had always wanted to sing like Ray Charles "but I think you had to be born with some kind of animal in your throat.")

"In New York, if you're friends with somebody, you walk up to him and you go 'Hey stooopid!' and he goes 'Hey jerk!' and you smack him. It means 'I love you, man!' But in California if I did that, they'd go like 'Oh wow. You're so *ho-stile!*' "

Within weeks, Joel had composed more than enough material for an album – but the recording of his third LP for Columbia was to prove a frustrating affair. He had recently switched management to Caribou, the organization run by James William Guercio and Larry Fitzgerald, and Guercio was lined up to produce the new album. Guercio, one-time bass player with The Dick Clark Road Show in the Sixties, had made his name in the early Seventies as the producer for the highly successful jazz-rock band Chicago, and, in 1973, he had opened his own Caribou ranch recording studio in California. In 1974 Elton John had recorded an album there – he named the record *Caribou* in the studio's honour – and his backing rhythm section had been drummer Nigel Olsson and bass player Dee Murray. Guercio had been greatly impressed with Olsson and Murray's studio performance and wanted to use them on the new Billy Joel album. This didn't seem too smart a move to Billy, however; in the past, he had been compared frequently and unfavourably with Elton John – if he used Elton's sidemen, he would just be confirming those comparisons. And yet, he didn't put up much

From left: Liberty DeVitto, Doug Stegmeyer, Billy Joel and Richie Cannata

of a fight to begin with: "I figured 'Who am *I* to argue with Jimmy Guercio. He's a big *mongo* in the music business.'"

So Joel, Olsson and Murray went into New York's Columbia studios with Jimmy Guercio and began to play around the new material, and it was immediately obvious, to Billy at least, that the trio just didn't cut the mustard as a musical team. Now convinced that the arrangement would never work, Billy went to his Columbia bosses and asked them to let him produce his album himself. They agreed. Reluctantly.

But Joel *would* produce the album. And he'd also use his own goddamned musicians on it for a change. He had by now recruited the rhythm section that would remain the nucleus of his backing bands over the coming years – Liberty DeVitto, a mad drummer who had once worked with the equally mad Mitch Ryder, and Long Island bass player Doug Stegmeyer. Doug and Liberty would become more than hired crony musicians, they would become Joel's close friends and they'd help to keep his "head together" whenever the going got weird: "The guys keep me in line," said Billy in 1978. "If I ever start acting like a rock star, Liberty'll come over and go 'Who do you think you *are*, you jerk?' It keeps me healthy. I don't like that arrogant 'I'm a rock star and I'm all punk and I'm great and everyone else stinks' attitude. And I can't have that arrogant attitude with Liberty watching me."

Liberty DeVitto would always be there with some clean, wholesome prank if needed. Driving cars into hotel lobbies, wearing phoney plastic moustaches on stage and writing alternative disgusting lyrics to Billy's songs – "honesty" becomes "sodomy" etc – have figured amongst his most fondly remembered stunts. But his "best" joke of all concerns Billy and Billy's father (who had been reunited in 1972 when Joel Sr. had been in California on business). When these two are together, and Liberty's there too, the drummer calls Billy "Herr Joel", and he calls Billy's dad *"No Herr Joel"*. Yes! Howard Joel is bald! And the fact that he doesn't understand Liberty's pun at all makes the joke even funnier. Life's a riot. But it wasn't always. The new Billy Joel album, *Turnstiles,* was released in May 1976, crept up the *Billboard* album chart as far as Number 122, and promptly flopped off into

oblivion. It was a commercial catastrophe. But quite *why* the LP proved to be such a market-place dud is hard to figure out. For *Turnstiles* was easily Billy Joel's most assured work yet – and *certainly* his most entertaining.

Only on two tracks, the twee McCartneyesque 'James', and 'Summer, Highland Falls', another Jackson Browne impersonation – so *uncannily* accurate this time that it might well have been intended as some elaborate joke – did Joel sound anything like the rather awkward and aimless "singer-songwriter" of *Streetlife Serenade*. The remaining six tracks were strong and varied and, for the first time, Billy Joel's music was afforded the treatment it deserved: the cast of 1,000 carefree sessioneers had gone; here was a bunch of *proper* backing musicians: DeVitto, Stegmeyer, guitarist Russell Stavors and multi-instrumentalist Richie Cannata (both of whom would become stalwarts of the B.Joel back-up crew). These men might not be as slick and polished as the Hollywood crew; they might even play quite a lot of wrong notes from time to time. But they had the *feeling* – and it showed, from the rattle and flourish of the album's opening cut, 'Say Goodbye To Hollywood', through to the stuttering power pop close of 'Miami 2017 (Seen The Lights Go Out On Broadway)' (not counting the pair of aforementioned stinky songs in between).

'Say Goodbye To Hollywood' was both a celebration of Joel's return from California and an exuberant tribute to the sound of Phil Spector and The Ronettes. And, in 1978, Ronnie Spector repaid the tribute with her own version of the song, much to Billy's delight: "When the *Turnstiles* album first came out there was a review in the *Village Voice* which really bugged me. The guy made a point of saying 'Say Goodbye To Hollywood' was a pathetic rip-off of Phil Spector and Ronnie Spector and Bruce Springsteen when what it actually was was a tribute to that Phil Spector sound. That review really ripped me up. But I had the last laugh on that guy 'cause it ended up with Ronnie Spector recording it and The E Street Band playing on it. So 'ha ha ha!'" (Meanwhile, Ronnie Spector was commenting: "When I heard the song, I said 'That's for me!' I love it – it reminds me a little

of my marriage. It's one hell of a song for a comeback for me.")

The mood of 'Miami 2017' was altogether different; here was a vision of something not very nice somewhere in the future, inspired by New York City's parlous financial state of 1975. "Gerald Ford made a speech saying he wasn't going to give federal aid to New York City and there was this headline in the paper: 'Ford To New York: Drop Dead!' And that sparked off this vision of being a grandfather in the year 2017, living in Miami Beach, talking to my grandchildren saying 'I remember what happened in New York City when the gunboats came up and blew the whole place away.'" And there were many other moods. There was the smoky, late-night soul crawl of 'New York State Of Mind', there was 'Angry Young Man', a strident attack on self-pity introduced by a prelude of ferocious hammering on the piano, and there was 'I've Loved These Days', a remarkable ballad of world-weariness and exhausted patience. "That was a commentary on the state of America having to settle for a lesser style of living," Billy recalled in 1979. "I hate to explain this but I really should. It was when the gas thing hit, the dollar went down, our influence in the world was shrinking – it was like 'You Americans have been pigs long enough. You're really gonna have to start cooling it.' That was what I was trying to get with that song – we live in luxury, I've *loved* these days but it's gonna stop. We can't live like this anymore. It's the end of an era." Serious business.

But it wasn't the "heavy" content of some of the album's concerns that prevented *Turnstiles* from being a success. What was it then? Reviews didn't help: *Creem* described Joel as "a Jackson Browne folkie at heart with Elton John-like pretensions. . . He continues to sing real-life soap opera songs that rarely show any signs of imagination." The reviewer went on to say that he had actually been to a Billy Joel concert once but had fallen asleep; and most other critics took this line – Billy Joel, the soppy-voiced plodder who thinks he's got something important to say. But then critics have never had *that* much effect on an album's sales; the critics didn't prevent FM radio stations from giving *Turnstiles* a fair deal of airplay. But still it crocked out.

Ronnie Spector would cover 'Say Goodbye To Hollywood' and so too, ironically enough, would Nigel Olsson. And 'New York State Of Mind' would be recorded by Barbra Streisand (such a celebrity legend that they just call her "Streisand"). Here was honour indeed. But as the summer of 1976 drew to a close, what Billy Joel needed far more than honours was a hit record. Money was not exactly raining down; in fact, it wasn't even drizzling. Joel had broken with Caribou but Caribou still owned a piece of him. Artie Ripp still owned various pieces of him. Billy didn't seem to have a piece of himself to call his own. He belonged to others, 150 per cent; the *Piano Man* album had been certified gold but, so far, Joel had received less than 8,000 dollars in royalties. What to do?

DISCOGRAPHY

STREETLIFE SERENADE *(1974)*

ONE SIDE
Streetlife Serenader
Los Angelenos
The Great Suburban Showdown
Root Beer Rag
Roberta

ANOTHER SIDE
The Entertainer
Last Of The Big Time Spenders
Souvenir
The Mexican Connection

ALL WORDS AND MUSIC: Billy Joel
PRODUCER: Michael Stewart
MUSICIANS: Gary Dalton/Richard Bennett/ Mike Deasy/Roj Rather/Al Hertzberg/Don Evans/Art Munson/Michael Stewart *(guitars);* Emory Gordy/Larry Knechtel/ Wilton Felder *(bass);* Ron Tutt *(drums);* Tom Whitehorse *(pedal steel/banjo);* Joe Clayton *(congas);* William Smith *(organ).*

SINGLES:
'The Entertainer'.

TURNSTILES (1976)

SIDE ONE
Say Goodbye To Hollywood
Summer, Highland Falls
All You Wanna Do Is Dance
New York State Of Mind

SIDE TWO
James
Prelude/Angry Young Man
I've Loved These Days
Miami 2017 (Seen The Lights Go Out On Broadway)

ALL WORDS AND MUSIC: Billy Joel
PRODUCER: Billy Joel
MUSICIANS: Liberty DeVitto *(drums);* Doug Stegmeyer *(bass);* Russell Javors/ Howie Emerson/James Smith *(guitars);* Richard Cannata *(sax);* Mingo Lewis *(percussion).*

SINGLES:
'Say Goodbye to Hollywood';
'James'.

6

FOR A PENNY YOU CAN BUY A BOOK OF MATCHES – AND SET YOURSELF ON FIRE

Billy was feeling the pressure from a lot of different sides, not the least being Columbia Records. After a couple of clinker albums – it had taken *Piano Man* more than two years to reach gold, *Streetlife Serenade* was a modest success at best, and *Turnstiles* was

❝ *Everybody's a little schizophrenic – even polyphrenic, I think. You think you know your friends, but then they start acting crazy and you go 'Hey Jocko! Who is this guy?' That's The Stranger.* **❞**

Billy Joel, 1984

an unqualified disaster – Billy was going to have to come up with a big hit. Although he later claimed that he really wasn't paying attention to the demands of the market-place after the failure of *Turnstiles,* he did admit to appreciating the fact that major record labels don't like to carry artists who don't produce big albums after the first or second outing and don't appreciate waiting around for their artists to hit. For every Bruce Springsteen, Boz Scaggs, or Bob Seger – artists for whom it took a couple of LPs to get going – there are thousands of forgotten bands and singers whose albums fill up the cut-out bins, never to be heard of again.

Aside from commercial failure, Billy had something even worse going for him. Because he had fired Jimmy Guercio from the *Turnstiles* sessions and produced the album himself, he had the reputation for being a hothead and a stupid one at that. As Billy put it: "I had left management, I had left California, I had a band I insisted on recording with. . .

When I told Jimmy 'This isn't going to work out, I'm going to produce this myself,' I'm sure in record company circles, a little red line went through my name. 'Oh, he's firing Jimmy Guercio and he's gonna produce it himself. OK, clunk, that's the end of him.' That was around the time when I had Elizabeth come in and do management. That was a double red line. 'Oh, he's going to produce it himself and his wife is going to manage him. OK, bye-bye Billy.' " Billy said that he had to take a stand and produce his own record, but it turned out to be a stumble.

Hiring Elizabeth was also a stand, but this, at least, turned out to be a good move. It was the result, according to Billy, of a casual remark: " 'Everything is a mess,' I said. 'Look, why don't you manage me? You know how dumb musicians can be and you've been hanging around me long enough.' " Then, as the story goes, the very next morning Elizabeth hired a secretary, had phone lines installed in their New York apartment and hired a booking agent to get Billy some lucrative concert dates. As Billy recalls: "Overnight, our home was turned into an office and I couldn't find a place to sit down. I was run out of my own house, so we called the new company Home Run." The arrangement was

met with scepticism from many quarters, but as Billy said: "I knew she was smart. If you can't trust your own wife to manage you, who can you trust? And I figured this will be the first case of Artist Screws Manager."

Elizabeth did a good job. She renegotiated Billy's contract with Columbia to get him a deal that gives him over a dollar a record. Home Run began a booking agency which insured that Billy could collect at least a couple of million dollars for a concert tour instead of a couple of thousand. And, in addition to managing Billy, Home Run became an umbrella corporation embracing music publishing, video and magazine publishing. As Elizabeth put it, one of the reasons she became so successful was that "people never expected me to be as smart as I was, and they would be totally frank because they didn't realize I was building my empire. They taught me that money is the bottom line of everything."

"I knew she was smart. If you can't trust your own wife to manage you, who can you trust? And I figured this will be the first case of Artist Screws Manager."

With his management taken care of, Billy set about finding a producer for the crucial upcoming LP. One night during that year's tour, Billy played a small venue in Glassboro, New Jersey. After that gig, Billy met with George Martin, The Beatles' producer, to discuss producing the album. With his love for The Beatles, Billy was thrilled to meet Martin and excited about the idea of working with him. But it wasn't to be. Apparently, Martin didn't like Billy's band. According to Billy: "He thought they were too rough, too street rock and roll unpolished. It was kind of disappointing, but once again I had to stick up for the band. I went back and they said, 'What did he say, what did he say?' I didn't want to tell the band that he didn't want to use you guys so I told them, 'Oh, I don't think it will work out, time schedules and bleh, bleh, bleh!' "

So, still stuck without a producer, Billy turned to Paul Simon's producer, Phil Ramone, a veteran of New York session work and an illustrious name in New York recording circles. Elizabeth set up the meeting, arranged the scheduling and made sure that Billy was available to work with Ramone. Billy had been eager to work with Ramone for a long time, but scheduling problems had prevented it. What really sold Billy on Phil Ramone, though, was the fact that he liked the band. As someone used to the slick, dour professionalism of old-time session men, Ramone was taken with the raw, "street" sound of the band and didn't want to change them at all. This was a big relief to Billy who noted, "Every time we worked with a producer, it was like the producer was testing them [the band]. They had been under the gun with other producers, having to prove themselves. Phil liked my guys right off the bat. He heard them play the songs and said, 'Don't play any different than you play on the road – be the rock 'n' roll animals that you are.' And that made the band play better." And so began the partnership that would change the course of Billy Joel's career.

"I didn't know I was going to call the album *The Stranger* when we went in. We didn't take a long time agonizing over the perfect take and the right way to do it. If it felt good, fine."

Billy and the band went into New York's A&R Recording Studio in early 1977 to begin work on *The Stranger*. Unlike the tortured experiences the recording of his previous LPs had been this album was a breeze. And although Billy had completed only three songs before recording began, *The Stranger* was finished in five weeks. The band worked together in the studio, improvising, putting bits together, with Billy either writing in the studio or bringing finished songs in the next day. It was "inspiring". "I didn't have a concept for the album," Billy told Ed Sciaky of WIOQ Radio in Philadelphia. "I didn't know I

58

was going to call the album *The Stranger*
when we went in. We didn't take a long time
agonizing over the perfect take and the right
way to do it. If it felt good, fine." Phil
Ramone's spontaneity was thrilling to Billy.
"He was one of the guys," Billy enthused.
"We'd throw around ideas, kick the songs
around, try them different ways and get them
tight. Sometimes we'd throw pizza at each
other. That's how it was with Phil. It's a
communal thing in the studio. It was inspiration! We created heat in the studio."

'Just The Way You Are', for example,
would never have become the standard it has
without Phil Ramone's uncanny knack for
finding new contexts and sounds for Billy's
material. Left to his own devices, Billy probably would have recorded the song as a
conventional slow rock ballad, but "Phil came
in and listened to it and he goes to Liberty
DeVitto, 'Why don't you play this backwards,
a samba?' Liberty's a real rock 'n' roll drummer. It's against every grain in his body to
play these samba-type beats, but he did it and
it seemed to flow along OK."

Instead of the usual ten to twenty takes
that had marred Billy's earlier recordings,
The Stranger's tracks were completed in five
or six. Billy recorded his vocals live at the
piano; he doesn't believe in overdubbing and
the LP was completed just in time for Billy
and the band to go out on tour again.

It is obvious, almost from first listening,
that *The Stranger* was the first time Billy had
ever really had fun in a recording studio. His
voice is stronger and less idiosyncratic than
on previous LPs, the band has got some
energy finally, and the songs are uniformly
strong. The new, liberated tone is set with the
very first track, 'Movin' Out (Anthony's
Song)'. Despite its annoying "ack ack ack ack
ack acks," the song is full of incident – Sgt.
O'Leary on his beat, Mama Leone's on Sullivan Street, houses in Hackensack, all people
and places well known to East Coast young
people. Despite its cynical and even bitter
rejection of day-to-day life, the song is still
affectionate and bouncy. 'The Stranger' is the
LP's centrepiece. The plaintive whistle which
opens the song, and closes the LP, was added
to the song when Billy realized: "There was
something missing. It needed a theme. And I
had this picture of like Humphrey Bogart

with his raincoat over his shoulder walking down a rain-drenched street in France. I did the whistling." The song has a distinctive, gritty piano riff, the perfect complement to the lyrics themselves – a revealing portrait of Billy's own inner confusion and complexity.

'Just The Way You Are' is, of course, the best known song on the album. Although Phil Woods' sax solo gives the song a warm, jazzy feel, Billy isn't overly fond of the piece. He once said: "The closest thing we ever got to artificial sound reproduction was. . .with those voices going "aaa," like on 10cc's 'I'm Not In Love', same effect. And we had to use a tape for that. I really don't like to do that." It was originally titled 'Don't Go Crazy'. Billy has said it's "a nice cover song, nothing more." Written as a birthday present for Elizabeth, the song has often been criticized as a sexist put-down – though this seems a little nit-picking, especially since Elizabeth, the song's muse, is far from a stay-at-home suburban drone.

'Scenes From An Italian Restaurant' was one of the first songs written for the LP and one that Billy told George Martin about because he saw it as a mini version of the second side of The Beatles' *Abbey Road*. The original title was 'The Ballad Of Brenda And Eddie', and the track goes through numerous rhythmic changes before it ends with its dramatic "Bottle of red/Bottle of white" finale. More than any other of Billy's compositions, 'Scenes' is a perfect picture of Long Island youth in the late Fifties and early Sixties – cheap taste, restlessness, low aspirations, ill-conceived marriages, feigned toughness, the whole American suburban dream Billy Joel knew so much – *too* much – about.

'Only The Good Die Young' is probably the most controversial song on the LP. One of Billy's teachers noted that Virginia was a girl in Billy's high school choral group with whom he had a less than satisfying time, and so the song becomes a semi boogie-woogie ode to teenage frustration. Its "Catholic girls start much too late" observation disturbed lots of people who took it to be anti-Catholic and the track was banned on radio stations across the country. Billy was once even threatened with assassination in St. Louis if he performed the song. He was so irritated: "I did it twice." The overblown reaction to such a harmless song

staggered him. Why, he thought, somewhat naively, can't people take a pinch of humour, now and then? "I'm always surprised by the lack of humour a lot of people show," he said in response to a question about the song. "I'm supposed to be bitter and cynical, but I think I'm making fun of things. I think I'm making a joke. I think it happens to be a New York kind of thing."

'She's Only A Woman' is another, much more sincere, melodic love song for Elizabeth. Another target for those who would like to accuse Billy of rampant chauvinism, the track is clearly about a complicated woman who is a contradictory amalgam of different aspects, moods and needs. The only inconsistency is that Elizabeth never did "get a degree."

Although *The Stranger* was to become the most successful record in Columbia Records' history, it took a while for it to catch on. Most of the buying public were doing the Latin Hustle to the strains of *Saturday Night Fever* – on its way to becoming one of the biggest records of all time – when *The Stranger*, hardly a record to win a dance contest with, was released. In addition, Columbia didn't handle the marketing of the record too well. Still casting Billy in the sensitive singer-songwriter mould, the initial ad copy for the record contained this bit of baffling prose: "The Stranger—he's the one who sits down next to you at the bar or on the plane or in the restaurant, and he tells you stories about somebody vaguely familiar. . .somebody you suddenly realize is yourself."

More appropriate for a *Twilight Zone* episode starring Harry Chapin, this kind of marketing didn't give The Bee Gees any sleepless nights. On top of that, the first single release was 'Movin' Out', an unwise choice because of its uniquely New York evocations and idiosyncratic vocals; the record bombed. However, FM stations, in a show of feisty independence that's unusual these days, started playing 'Just The Way You Are' instead of the prescribed single and noticed dramatically positive feedback on the tune. In response, Columbia released the single six weeks after 'Movin' Out'.

Critical response was also lackadaisical. Although he was headlining Nassau Coliseum at the time, Billy was still a second or

third tier artist who didn't warrant the lead reviews and media attention he'd get later. In *Rolling Stone*, a newsy sort of review, three or four pages into the review section, said: "We don't expect subtlety or understatement from him and indeed his lyrics can be as smart-assed as ever. But Ramone's emphasis on sound definitely lessens the impact of the sarcasm, which in the long run may help boost Joel's career immeasurably. In the meantime, old fans will have to listen more carefully than usual. . . Together with producer Phil Ramone, Joel has achieved a fluid sound occasionally sparked by a light soul touch. It is a markedly different effect than his pound-it-out-to-the-back-rows concert flash."

In spite of the critical boredom and offbeat advertising, 'Just The Way You Are' began climbing the charts, carrying *The Stranger* on its coat-tails. Billy, however, was on tour, apparently not listening to the radio or reading the trades, so it took a while for his burgeoning success to sink in. "We were seeing younger kids come in and older people and all sorts of people and they were recognising the new material much quicker than people had picked up on the older stuff," he remembered. "That's when we recognised that something must be going on. I guess it was sort of a surprise."

In September 1977, Billy performed 'Just The Way You Are' on *Saturday Night Live* for an estimated audience of 20 million viewers (causing him to miss his 10th high school anniversary) – at a time when SNL was "must" viewing for anyone with any socks – and he was well on his way to becoming a household word. By the end of 1978, four singles were taken from the LP, all of which made the *Billboard* charts; even the reissue of 'Movin' Out' squirmed to the Top Twenty. 'Just The Way You Are' won two Grammys, "Record Of The Year" and "Song Of The Year". Billy was finally there.

DISCOGRAPHY

THE STRANGER
(December 1977)

SIDE ONE
Movin' Out (Anthony's Song)
The Stranger
Just The Way You Are
Scenes From An Italian
  Restaurant

SIDE TWO
Vienna
Only The Good Die Young
She's Always A Woman
Get It Right The First Time
Everybody Has A Dream

ALL WORDS AND MUSIC: Billy Joel
PRODUCER: Phil Ramone
MUSICIANS: Liberty DeVitto *(drums);* Doug Stegmeyer *(bass);* Richard Cannata *(sax/clarinet/flute/organ);* Steve Khan/ Hiram Bullock *(guitars);* with: David Brown/Hugh McCracken/Steve Burgh *(guitars);* Phil Woods *(sax);* Ralph MacDonald *(percussion);* Richard Tee *(organ);* Dominic Cortese *(accordian).*

SINGLES:
'Just The Way You Are';
'Movin' Out (Anthony's Song)';
'Only The Good Die Young';
'She's Always A Woman'.

7

ONE MORE KAMIKAZE

In early 1978, Joel entered New York's A&R Recording Studio once more to work on the follow-up album to *The Stranger*. Having at last established a reputation for himself, he now had to consolidate it – a lot to ask and, deliberately, he avoided thinking about it: "When we were recording *52nd Street*, one of the main things we avoided talking about was 'Well, is this going to be as successful as *The Stranger?*' Because you could drive yourself crazy thinking like that. The record company might be thinking like that but I just wanted to put out a *good* record. *Stranger II* or *Son Of Stranger?* That would be boring. I wanted to explore my own potential."

Nonetheless, the new LP was created in much the same way as its predecessor, the songs springing forth easily and spontaneously, and the recording process seeming more of a pleasure than a grind. Released in September, the album was an immediate success, selling an astonishing three million copies within a month and making Number 1 on the *Billboard* charts. *52nd Street* received critical acclaim too; it got the lead review in *Rolling*

> **"** *The biggest issue right now as far as I'm concerned is inflation. I never go shopping but I went to the supermarket the other day and a quart of milk was like 55 cents... It smacks of the Weimar Republic. This is the United States of America! How can this happen? Look at it this way. Take a country, an African country. They don't want the new General Electric Squeezin' Art Fruit Smasher, they just want the fruit.* **"**

Billy Joel, 1979

> **"** *Don't take any shit from anybody!* **"**

Billy Joel, 1978, 1979, 1980, 1981, 1982. . .

Stone and a long one at that – an involved piece by Stephen Holden on Joel's place in the pantheon of Seventies' superstars. Comparing him to pretty much everyone from George Gershwin through George M. Cohan, Cole Porter, Sammy Davis Jr., Anthony Newley and Bob Dylan to The Beatles, Holden asserted that "Joel is very much a phenomenon of the times: an urban realist in the age of gossip-mongering and the sinking dollar, a cynical ultra-professional in a booming culture racket, the artistic standards of which are now determined by mass-market technologies. Neither a great singer, nor a great writer, Billy Joel is a great show business personality in the tradition of Al Jolson. He's every scuffling city boy who ever made it big, crowing with ego but also giving back his all. . . The result is as perfect and flattering a studio presentation as can be imagined." Phew.

It was this sort of high-falutin' talk that bothered Billy, however. No, he wasn't Cole Porter or Al Jolson; nor was he a Tin Pan Alley hack, sipping champagne in elegant townhouses, sending a single rose to the society babe who had broken his heart by dancing with another feller at the Stork Club. He was a rock and roller, more like Bruce Springsteen than Oscar Levant. But Holden and others can't be chided for seeing Billy Joel as a pop style stylist, for *52nd Street* was, undoubtedly, his most sophisticatedly urban

---

"I can't take my piano into the Holiday Inn. If I try to write lyrics on the road, I always find myself saying 'Oh, here I am at the Holiday Inn. Another empty bottle and another tale to tell.' I really don't like that kind of road song. There have been too many written. I think Holiday Inn should pay songwriters for plugging them."

– and jazziest – album so far, made up of grand ballads like 'Until The Night', a tribute to (or, as Billy has admitted, a "rip off" of) The Righteous Brothers, and 'Honesty', a simple and unpretentious vocal work-out in his McCartney style, which was one of the few songs he's ever written on the road. ("I have a hard time writing on the road," Billy has said. "Number one – I'm not a guitarist. A guitar player can take his guitar to his hotel room but I can't take my piano into the Holiday Inn. Number two – if I try to write lyrics on the road, I always find myself saying 'Oh, here I am at the Holiday Inn. Another empty bottle and another tale to tell.' I really don't like that kind of road song. There have been too many written. I think Holiday Inn should pay songwriters for plugging them.")

Then there was 'Big Shot', on which Billy played the snotty-nosed brat; the song was a childish put-down of someone showing off for their friends and making a fool of themselves trying to be sophisticated. "The song is about anybody who has ever had a hangover," Billy said at the time. "Wake up in the morning

and you can't move and you're so hung over, saying 'You stupid idiot. You had to be a big shot.' I did a lot of personal research for that song. . ."

And then, of course, there was 'My Life' which, more than any other of his numbers, has become Billy Joel's signature tune, a brash statement of independence and self-assertion. "I wrote 'My Life' as a bar song," Joel told the authors in 1984. "I pictured a whole bunch of people sitting at a bar and turning around and raising their glasses and going 'I don't care what you say anymore this is MY LIFE!!' It's like parents saying to their kids 'Get outta the house, already!' " (Originally, however, the song had been just a restrained boom-da-boom piano hook with no accompanying words: "The turnaround part of the song was the first part that was written and I couldn't find words for it so Liberty came up with these *obscene* lyrics – 'You *hmmmmm* my *hmmmmm* – what a way to say good morning'. . .Use your imagination!")

Unlike some of his other LPs, *52nd Street* had a consistent tone and feel, none of the tracks clashed or sounded out of place. In short, a smart piece of work – and the LP picked up two Grammys: "Album Of The Year" and "Male Vocal Performance Of The Year". Although Billy had attended the Grammy Awards ceremony the previous year – 'Just The Way You Are' had won "The Song Of The Year" category – he decided not to attend in 1979. At first he joked that maybe he should have sent an Indian representative, in imitation of Marlon Brando's famous non-acceptance of his Academy Award for *The Godfather,* but decided not to go because "it was too Vegasy. It means putting on a tux and 'thanking all the little people.' " Phil Ramone went as Billy's stand-in and provided the only amusing moment in the proceedings. The ceremony that year resembled a revival meeting more than a forum for "the industry to honour its own." Artist after artist, from a newly-born-again Bob Dylan, to praise-the-Lord Donna Summer, all thanked God for their talent. After several such acceptance speeches, it was a breath of fresh air when a mordant Ramone accepted Billy's award with the wry observation, "I guess the Lord must live in New York City." Billy couldn't have done better himself.

A boy, his girl and his bike

Billy and his bodyguard at a screening of Reds

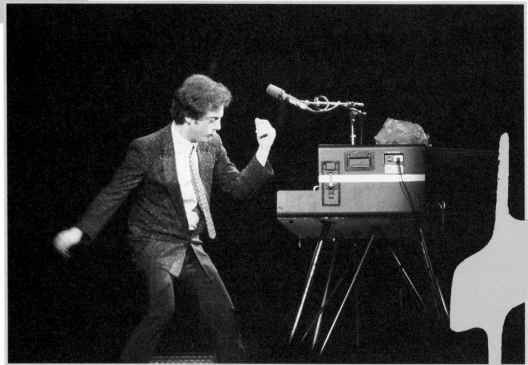

And at the end of the night he leaves you with a simple, understandable adieu – "Don't take any shit from anybody!" he yells. Don't let the bastards grind you down. The crowds yell back in appreciation . . .

On the road again in 1979, Billy Joel was selling out 20,000-seat arenas across the United States. And anyone who went to one of his concerts expecting some sort of Barry Manilow schmaltz-in was sure to be disappointed. Billy has observed that many concert-goers come to his shows expecting to hear endless variations on his mellower ballads only to be dismayed when they hear the sound turned up loud, see Liberty DeVitto pounding his drums like a man demented (which, of course, he is), Doug Stegmeyer abusing his bass and watch Billy himself belting out his songs on the up-tempo and gyrating wildly across the width of the stage on his stumpy, hyperactive legs. At a BJ concert you can see entire families shaking their groove "thangs" for their own very good reasons – because this is HIT music with rock PUNCH for the kids and a wholesome night OUT for mom and dad. Billy Joel is one of the guys. He's no faggot, he's not weird, he doesn't wear make-up, he doesn't travel around in limousines too much, he doesn't go to Africa to uncover the rhythmic schema of obscure Bantu tribes. On top of that, he wears a simple shirt, tie and jeans. He's just another lower-middle-class boy who got lucky and hasn't let success go to his head. He dishes out simple rock'n'roll and you have a good time. And at the end of the night he leaves you with a simple, understandable adieu – "Don't take any shit from anybody!" he yells. Don't let the bastards grind you down. The crowds yell back in appreciation . . .

One of Billy's less "orthodox" concert appearances of 1979 was in March at the Havana Jam, a series of concerts organized by CBS (Columbia's parent company) in Cuba. The other artists included Kris Kristofferson, Rita Coolidge, Stephen Stills, Weather Re-

port and John McLaughlin, not a particularly exciting line-up, and Billy was chosen to end the show. He received the only standing ovation of the series, and the mostly-Cuban crowd rushed the stage at the end of the set.

Billy had decided on the Cuban date for several reasons. Because his father had lived briefly in the country on his way to America, Billy was interested in seeing the place. He also had a genuine curiosity about the country since it is definitely forbidden fruit for most Americans; and since the band had just done a tour of northern Europe in the dregs of winter, they were eager to catch some Caribbean rays before heading home to the equally dismal northeast.

However, just as the Joel entourage arrived in Havana, Billy and Elizabeth discovered that CBS was planning to record the concert for release as an LP. Billy refused; or, more to the point, Elizabeth refused.

There were several reasons for this refusal. The first was ideological, or something. Since none of the Cubans at the concert or anywhere else in the country were going to be able to buy the record, Billy felt their presence shouldn't be exploited to fill CBS's coffers. The other reason was explained by Billy in *Playboy* a few years after the fact: "We weren't going to be on a record we had no control over. We were not going to help bail CBS out for what it spent on this thing and rip off the Cuban people. We were there to play, not to exploit it. Then all those stories came out about how we ruined it for everybody because we wouldn't let them tape our part of the show. The stories said that Elizabeth was giving everybody a hard time and we were prima donnas. Well, that's the press again."

Billy was surprised that the Cuban audience knew his music, but then was informed that since Cubans can pick up Miami stations, they knew a lot about American hits. His report of the concert is entertaining: "Stephen Stills came out and made this big speech about *Viva La Revolución* in Spanish. And the audience just kind of went 'We've been hearing this stuff all our lives. We don't need to hear this.' They came to hear rock and roll. Now, I know that critics like Robert Palmer don't consider me rock and roll – he thinks I'm the new Neil Diamond or some-

thing – but we played a rock and roll show. The only thing I said on stage was, 'No hablo Español,' then went into 'Big Shot' and the place went like whaa."

At the end of 1979, Billy went into the studio to record *Glass Houses* and, as the album was being released, Billy toured Europe, including a stop in Israel on the tour itinerary. "We'll go to the Wailing Wall, bring out guitars and start wailing," he joked before he made the trip. The visit brought him some flack from European journalists who equated playing Israel with the advocation of international Fascism. Billy stood up in Turin to say "I played in Israel for the same reason I played in Cuba – to play for the people. We wanted to see what the people in Israel were like instead of listening to the propaganda we get in our country." He got a standing ovation, but that was the last time he would have such an easy time with the press.

1980 was the year the American rock establishment discovered and exploited "new wave" music the way they had jumped on the disco bandwagon in '78 and '79 (in other words, a year or two after these new "movements" had sprung up). Punk, and its bastard (though better-behaved) child, "new wave", in addition to shocking the music industry out of a seven- or eight-year complacency, also carried along with it an insistence on rock credentials, a return to street credibility. The rock aristocracy, who had assumed for years that their hold on the affections and pocketbooks of the audience was secure, were suddenly challenged by bands like The Ramones, The Sex Pistols, The Clash and others who spat in the face of fleshy superstardom, indulgent over-production and banal songwriting. Extravagant art rock, as practised by such stalwarts as The Electric Light Orchestra, Emerson Lake and Palmer and Yes, was no longer acceptable to the best and brightest music fans. They wanted the real, sweaty thing, with lots of Farfisa organ, *if* you please.

Paul Simon, not a bombastic superstar, but the most effective and affecting and talented of the singer-songwriters, took 1979 to make *One Trick Pony*, a semi-autobiographical film which included his days as a street singer and Brill Building composer. The hit single from that film's soundtrack, 'Late In The Evening', was his most energetic work ever and told the musical story of his life from subway stations to first love. Linda Ronstadt, never shy about picking up on a trend, released an LP entitled *Mad Love* in 1980. The twist was that instead of using her usual sessionmen – mellow southern California studio vets who appeared on most of the LPs recorded by the LA mafia – she went "new wave" and picked up a local club band, The Cretones, who provided her with what she thought was Madame Wong credibility.

Billy Joel was also influenced by the sounds coming out of London and the Lower East Side. He told Timothy White: "If I'm considered part of that over-hyped, over-produced, over-indulgent supergroup style, then I'm bummed. But I do admit that some of my earlier albums had that quality. What I'm saying. . .is that I happen to like Donna Summer's hits. . . As for new wave, I think it's good and necessary. Kick out the Emerson Lake and Palmer shit and all that over-indulgence. Give the whole damned industry an enema, jam that plastic tube right up its rear end."

If that's what Billy Joel thought he was doing with *Glass Houses* and the Number 1 hit from the record, 'It's Still Rock And Roll To Me', he wasn't given much time to wonder if he had succeeded or not. The response to that album was vicious. Paul Nelson in *Rolling Stone* couldn't contain his contempt for Billy. Comparing the record unfavourably even to *Mad Love*, Nelson wrote: "At any rate, since *Mad Love* and *Glass Houses*, MOR rock by superstars will surely sell millions of copies, perhaps a new music-biz trophy is in order. Let's award Billy Joel a polyester record and hope he'll go away. . . I guess what Joel's trying to do here is picture himself as a lovable loony, a teddy bear with a zip gun, but this brand of madness is snug enough – and smug enough – to make someone like Art Garfunkel look like Iggy Pop." The review doesn't let up, calling Joel a brat and singles' bar lounge lizard and winds up by observing . . . "what his defenders say is true: his material's catchy. But then, so's the flu." Jay Cocks, a *Time* critic (bearing in mind his reputation as a true rock spirit) said ". . .the music sounds like Broadway without a book and the lyrics are full of the backhand arrogance that Joel mistakes for true rock spirit. Midway through side two, Billy backs off and decides to flash his cosmopolitan credentials by trying a lyric in French. He isn't fluent in that language either." At the end of the year, the *Rolling Stone* Critic's Award honoured 'It's Still Rock And Roll To Me' as the worst song ever written about rock music.

Billy's intentions in making *Glass Houses* were clear. He was sick of people thinking he was MOR and wanted to "throw a rock at the image people have of me as a mellow balladeer." The title and cover, Billy throwing a rock at a glass house (which, incidentally, is his own house) on the front only to appear from behind the broken glass on the back, was a very deliberate statement. "It felt like a good idea," Billy said in early 1980. "Me with my tie thing on the back, staring through the hole that I made on the front cover throwing the rock. I'm throwing a rock at myself. Throwing stones at myself. Throwing rock and roll at myself. It's better than throwing it at other people." In keeping with the new establishment bid for rock cred above all else (this applied to critics as well as performers in a lot of cases), Billy said: "We've been playing rock and roll for years and years and years. This album is hard rock heavy. No balance between the ballads and the harder stuff." Billy was excited about making rock, nothing but rock, "Rock and roll seems to be making a comeback. . .Jazz went away and never came back, but rock and roll every fifteen years refreshes itself, cuts away all the extraneous stuff and goes back to the basics. And I think that's really good. Whether it's called new wave or no wave or, blah blah blah. . . When we were doing this album we got a couple of comments, 'What are you doing, new wave?' No, it's just rock and roll."

As for the genesis of the notorious song itself, it came about the same way that most of Billy's songs do; a little something comes into his head, someone else in the band picks up on it, pressuring him to finish the number. "I wanted to do a ten-song album," Billy said, discussing *Glass Houses*. "And we had nine and I needed one more. And I wrote it on the way to the studio. I was sitting in the back of the car with Doug Stegmeyer and I'm going 'Da da de da da. But it's all rock 'n' roll – no it's just rock 'n' roll – no, I had just the way

you are. It's only rock 'n' roll – no, The Stones did that – it's still rock 'n' roll.' And Doug was going, 'Nah, it still doesn't make it.' But I stuck with it 'cause when we got to the studio the band was gathered round the piano saying, 'What are we gonna do today, push ups?'"

It's as simple as that. For all the huffing and puffing that people read into 'It's Still Rock And Roll To Me', someone more familiar with Billy's music can see that it's not a radical departure from anything he's done in the past. It's full of the strutting that Billy often allows himself; but people were offended by it because Billy Joel IS NOT ROCK AND ROLL, HE'S POP. But, as Billy pointed out, he always played rock and roll, people just considered him pop because all they seemed to know were his ballads and slow numbers – the triumvirate of 'Piano Man', 'Captain Jack' and 'Just The Way You Are'. For Billy, these were just songs in his repertoire, which in his mind took equal billing with 'Say Goodbye To Hollywood', 'Big Shot', and 'My Life', Billy's rockier numbers. As he said: "When The Beatles did 'Yesterday', did that mean that they became an adult contemporary group suitable only for dentists' offices? No, that didn't stop them from doing any of the trashy rock and roll stuff they did. Same thing with The Stones. They did 'Angie' and 'Ruby Tuesday', but it didn't mean they weren't The Stones any more or had deserted their audience." So when Billy says "It's the next phase, new wave, dance craze/ It's still rock and roll to me," he's not belligerently stealing the rock mantle from pretenders to the throne, he's only saying that he likes rock music and that it includes him too.

If only Billy hadn't written that song, people wouldn't have got so hot and bothered about *Glass Houses*. Although not his most successful LP, it is not the unmitigated, offensive disaster it was made out to be. Even if there are some concessions to "stripped down sound," there are still plenty of ballads on the record, much the same œuvre Billy's always offered. The guitar *is* featured more prominently on a few numbers like 'It's Still. . .', 'You May Be Right' and 'Sometimes A Fantasy', but the piano is up there for all to all to hear on 'C'était Toi', 'All For Lenya' and 'Don't Ask Me Why'. 'Just A Fantasy' has a sound reminiscent of The Cars, particularly in its opening moments – Billy even apes Ric Ocasek's hiccough vocals – and 'You May Be Right' was an attempt at revisionist Sixties' pop that was popular at the turn of the decade, a form that Blondie was never particularly chastized for adopting. 'All For Lenya' though, is the album's *tour de force,* an epic in the tradition of 'Captain Jack', despite its organ break, about teenage obsessional love. If there's one major complaint to be made about *Glass Houses,* it's that it's hopelessly juvenile, more than any of Billy's other records. Although he calls himself a man in 'Lenya' and although 'C'était Toi' is clearly about an adult situation, most of the songs are about teenage problems and emotions. They are told without irony, as if they're accurate accounts of Billy's state of mind, so that the pronouncements about craziness and rock and roll ring untrue.

But if the album reviews were tough going, they were nothing compared to the stick that Billy got on his tour. The most notorious incident occurred in Los Angeles in August. Billy was playing a couple of nights in town and his show was reviewed by Ken Tucker of the LA *Herald Examiner* who called Billy "the great spoiled brat of rock, totally obsessed with himself. Last night he hopped all over the stage in a sustained fit of self-glory. He has always been a megalomaniac." According to a report in the *New York Post* a few days later: "Well, the singer went into a 'state of shock and absolute unbelief that anyone would *dare* attack him in such a way.' According to a member of his entourage, Joel 'stomped his feet, banged his fist, and behaved like a three-year-old that had dropped his jelly sandwich upside-down on the floor.' " The next night Billy brought the review on stage with him and referred to it constantly during the course of the set. At the end of the show he ripped the review to shreds, as the audience applauded, and shouted: "Fuck you, Ken Tucker."

Aside from problems with the critics, Billy had legal problems in 1980 and was forced to settle out of court in Nevada with a Reno songwriter, John Powers, who had sued Billy for stealing the copyright on 'My Life'. Powers claimed that he had submitted a song to the American Song Festival in 1974 entitled 'We Got To Get It Together' which Billy had turned into his own composition. Phil Ramone had been the A&R director at that festival; Powers also claimed that he had submitted the song on his own to CBS Records – all of which meant that Billy had had access to his song. Although there has never been official confirmation on the exact amount of the settlement, the *Reno Evening Gazette* and *Nevada State Journal* reported the figure to be close to 50,000 dollars. The incident infuriated Billy, who was still angry about it in 1982 when he discussed the suit with *Playboy:* "When I heard about it, I said, 'Let's go to court. Let's kill him. I want to *kill him.*' " Billy's lawyers convinced him that the case was unwinnable – a matter of song expert against song expert, and that the best course of action was not to terrorize a "shlump" from Reno who would have the Reno jury on his side. The lawyers suggested settling quietly. "But by the agreement," Billy related, "we were supposed to get a letter saying that I did not steal his song. I was totally against it, but I went along with the lawyers for once. So I'm supposed to have this letter. I've never seen this letter. And I hear that the guy does an act now and says, 'This is a song I wrote that Billy Joel stole.' Somebody else was going to sue me for another song. . .When I heard about it, I said 'No more of this settling shit.' If somebody sues, you have to countersue. Tell the guy, 'I'm going to countersue you for every penny you ever make, and I'll give it all to charity. I don't want your stinking money. You go after me, I'll kill you.' I never stole nobody's song. I'm still mad at the lawyers for letting me settle. It sucks."

Billy had often said that he would never make a live album because "We've recorded live and it doesn't knock me out. A lot of people record live albums as filler, to fill in the time between albums. When you're live, there's only one guy who's got his hand on the volume controls, and that's the sound man. It just doesn't come across the same. If I'm going to put out a live album, it's gonna be something special, something unique besides being a live album."

Songs In The Attic – Billy's live album, released in 1981 in between projects – strays from the usual live LP in that it's not an

On the stage of the Rex Cinema, Paris, April 1980

New York Yankees Bobby Murcer, Jim Spender and Ron Guidry meet Billy at Madison Square Garden

Billy leaves the US District Court in Brooklyn after testifying at the trial of Sam Goody Inc.

inferior version of a 'Greatest Hits' album, with one or two new studio tracks added on to give the album something tantalizing. None of Billy's big hits are on *Songs*. Rather, the eleven tracks are taken from *Cold Spring Harbor,* which no one had ever heard recorded properly, and from Billy's pre-*Stranger* recorded work. According to the review Timothy White wrote in *Rolling Stone:* "The resurrected past says a lot about Billy Joel's future: he won't go changing to try and please us. We'll have to take him just the way he is. *Songs In The Attic* is a reprise of miniatures and night moves made by Joel on the way to tempering the best of the music he hears in his head. . . A very careful edit of his scuffling days." Other positive reviews led Billy to think: "I must be doing something wrong."

One of the causes Billy felt very strongly about in 1981 was bootlegging, which was reaching epic proportions, and he decided to help the Justice Department in its anti-bootlegging campaign. "People who bought them [bootleg T-shirts] were getting ripped off and these guys were using my name to do it. I decided to try to stop them. When I did, the papers came out like I was trying to close down the little guys. The millionaire is trying to put these little guys out of business. But it has nothing to do with money. I've just spent too much time trying to hone my craft and I'm not going to have it watered down by somebody else's greed."

In March, in a case that received national attention, Billy testified as a government witness in the US Justice Department's trial against Sam Goody, one of the major record chains in the country, and one of its vice-presidents, Samuel Stolon. Stolon was ultimately found guilty by the New York jury of knowingly purchasing 23,000 counterfeit copies of the cassette version of the *Grease* soundtrack, while the Goody Corporation was convicted of infringing the copyright of *The Stranger* and the *Thank God It's Friday* soundtrack LP. The original indictment, however, charged that Stolon and four other men had "devised and executed" a plan to buy, sell and ship illegally copied tapes whose worth was estimated at more than one million dollars, including *Saturday Night Fever, Grease, Thank God It's Friday, The Stranger,* Andy Gibb's *Flowing Rivers* and Eric Clap-

ton's *Slowhand.* The indictment was dropped when the four co-defendants wound up as government witnesses in exchange for immunity from prosecution.

As eager as Billy was to help convict the bootleggers who were losing him and other artists thousands of dollars in royalties, he didn't help the case much. According to accounts of Billy's day in court, he chewed gum, mumbled his answers and couldn't distinguish between the authorized and bootlegged versions of *The Stranger* when they were played for him. He left the courthouse looking embarrassed and chagrined.

DISCOGRAPHY

52nd STREET (September 1978)

SIDE ONE
Big Shot
Honesty
My Life
Zanzibar

SIDE TWO
Stiletto
Rosalinda's Eyes
Half A Mile Away
Until The Night
52nd Street

ALL WORDS AND MUSIC: Billy Joel
PRODUCER: Phil Ramone
MUSICIANS: Liberty DeVitto *(drums);*
Doug Stegmeyer *(bass);* Richard Cannata
(sax); Steve Khan/David Spinozza/Hugh
McCracken/Eric Gale *(guitars);* Ralph
McDonald/David Friedman/Mike Mainieri
(percussion); Freddie Hubbard *(trumpet);*
George Marge *(recorder).*

SINGLES:
'My Life';
'Big Shot';
'Honesty';
'Until The Night'.

GLASS HOUSES (March 1980)

SIDE ONE
You May Be Right
Sometimes A Fantasy
Don't Ask Me Why
It's Still Rock'n'Roll To Me
All For Lenya

SIDE TWO
I Don't Want To Be Alone
Sleeping With The Television On
C'Etait Toi (You Were The One)
Close To The Borderline
Through The Long Night

ALL WORDS AND MUSIC: Billy Joel
PRODUCER: Phil Ramone

MUSICIANS: Liberty DeVitto *(drums);*
Doug Stegmeyer *(bass);* Russell Javors
(guitar); David Brown *(guitar);* Richard
Cannata *(sax, organ).*

SINGLES:
'All For Leyna';
'You May Be Right';
'It's Still Rock'n'Roll To Me';
'Don't Ask Me Why';
'Sometimes A Fantasy'.

SONGS IN THE ATTIC (September 1981)

SIDE ONE
**Miami 2017 (Seen The Lights Go Out On
Broadway)** (recorded at: Madison Square
Garden, New York)
Summer, Highland Falls (Bijou,
Washington D.C.)
Streetlife Serenader
(St Paul Civic Centre, St Paul, Minnesota)
Los Angelenos (Toad's Place, New Haven,
Connecticut)
She's Got A Way (Paradise Club, Boston,
Massachusetts)
Everybody Loves You Now (Bijou,
Washington D.C.)

SIDE TWO
Say Goodbye To Hollywood (Milwaukee
Arena, Wisconsin)
Captain Jack (Spectrum, Philadelphia,
Pennsylvania)
You're My Home (Bijou, Washington D.C.)
The Ballad Of Billy The Kid (Madison
Square Garden, New York)
I've Loved These Days (Horizon, Chicago,
Illinois)

ALL WORDS AND MUSIC: Billy Joel
PRODUCER: Phil Ramone
MUSICIANS. Liberty DeVitto *(drums);*
Doug Stegmeyer *(bass);* Russell Javors
(guitar); David Brown *(guitar);* Richard
Cannata *(sax/organ).*

SINGLES:
'Say Goodbye To Hollywood';
'She's Got A Way';
'You're My Home'.

8

KEEPING THE FAITH

> *I don't see how people have the audacity to call themselves artists. Vincent Van Gogh — that's an artist. Just to call yourself an artist because you're a musician, that's ridiculous. I can't be a plumber. My toilet breaks down and it really gets honky. What am I gonna do? Go in my bathroom and sing? No, I need a plumber. Plumber comes over and fixes my toilet. It works beautiful. It hasn't broken down in twenty-five years. So that plumber's an artist.*
>
> **Billy Joel, 1979**

By the end of 1981, Billy Joel had become a very rich, very successful "artiste"; and yet he was derided by the critical elite as a schmaltzy *schmuck* – a fact that continued to anger and depress him. For all his vehement insistence that he was a rock'n'roller at heart, it was for his tuneful ballads that he was best known and his public image had become that of a Neil Diamond/Barry Manilow-type entertainer, a singer of tear-jerking love melodies aimed at the hearts and the handkerchiefs of the ladies. The fact that such MOR superstars as Frank Sinatra and Barbra Streisand had covered his songs, that 'Just The Way You Are' and 'My Life' had become standards in the repertoires of countless club comedians and charmless cocktail-bar singers, hadn't helped. Nor had *Glass Houses,* his attempt to be taken seriously as a modern rock performer; the critical establishment had poured scorn on the album and, to add insult to injury, the frolicsome, squeaky-voiced kids cartoon group, The Chipmunks, had done a version of 'You May Be Right' on their *Chipmunk Punk* LP that knocked spots off the original. (Yes, the same Chipmunks whom Joel had complained of sounding like back in 1971 when his *Cold Spring Harbor* album had been mastered at the wrong speed. Cruel irony.) And then there had been his court appearance in the Sam Goody record-counterfeiting trial for which he had been widely ridiculed within the record business. Apart from selling millions of records, Billy Joel could do no right.

"I heard the other day that I was gay," Billy had said back in 1979. "I was in a club somewhere and this girl came up and said 'Is it true that you're gay?' She'd read it somewhere. What are you supposed to do? Beat up five guys and rape a couple of women? But I heard Burt Reynolds on a show once and he said 'You know you've made it when they start saying you're gay.'" But by the end of 1981 no one was calling Billy Joel gay, they were calling him mister clean, middle-of-the-road superstar, a Tin Pan Alley tunesmith, which was much worse. He had been described as "the ultimate in mediocrity." "If Bruce Springsteen had his balls chopped off, this is how he'd sound;" "Take your self-serving, self-righteous anger, Billy, and stick it where the sun don't shine;" "Joel's music, the 'I-coulda-

been-a-contender' whinings of a wimp" had been just a few of the many scathing remarks to appear in print in the early Eighties. Critic Robert Palmer, in a review of a 1980 Madison Square Garden concert, remarked that "Billy Joel has about as much to do with rock and roll as Beethoven had with a sneeze." And for all his defensiveness – saying things like "Debussy? He came on and people threw cabbages at him – and tomatoes" – Joel could not disguise the fact that all this adverse criticism wounded him. He read his notices and they hurt: "I'll read one and feel 'Aw man, not in front of all my friends, my relatives, my own ego for the damned *world* to see!' "

"I heard the other day that I was gay. I was in a club somewhere and this girl came up and said 'Is it true that you're gay?' She'd read it somewhere. What are you supposed to do? Beat up five guys and rape a couple of women?"

And yet the negative press didn't prevent millions of people from buying his records and enjoying his music, so why should he *care* what people wrote about him? Why did he let it wound him so? Just like The Stranger – his schizophrenic, "even polyphrenic" everyman – Billy Joel was full of contradictions. On the one hand, he'd be humble about his work, claiming that he was nothing special, just damned lucky to be making a living as a musician when there were a million other piano players out there who'd never be able to quit their day jobs. On the other, he wanted appreciation from the public and the critics alike. He wanted to be understood. Another contradiction: Billy Joel was just an ordinary, regular guy, he always said. He felt more at home in grungy bars talking to strangers about the New York Yankees than he did rubbing shoulders with fellow rock celebrities. And yet he wanted to be accepted as part of the musical fraternity and was surprised,

and a little hurt, that so few of his contemporaries had ever asked him to appear on their records.

Since becoming a big seller, Joel had performed on a mere handful of records by other artists. In 1976, he had lined up with a team of Long Island veterans (including Carmine Appice, once of Vanilla Fudge, and Leslie West, ex-Vagrants) and assorted music stars (Joe Cocker, Keith Moon, Roger McGuinn) on Bo Diddley's *20th Anniversary* LP, and that same year he joined a massive cast of around 40 back-up singers (everyone from Johnny Cash through Leonard Cohen to Joan Baez) on Earl Scruggs' *Anniversary Special* album. His few other sessions in the late Seventies and early Eighties had included a spot on *Night Lights,* an album by his one-time rival from Garden City, Elliot Murphy, work with keyboard player Bob James and with David Sanborn (on an instrumental version of Lou Reed's 'Walk On The Wild Side'), and a singing role on a D.L.Byron single – a version of Billie Joe Royal's 1965 hit 'Down In The Boondocks'.

Hardly prestigious stuff, any of it. "Nobody asks me," Billy was to complain in 1982: Maurice White, of Earth Wind & Fire, had once asked Joel to work with him, but nothing came of that. Eric Clapton had once called Billy up to enlist his musical services for a record "but he didn't get back to me." And then there had been Michael Jackson, who rang Billy to suggest recording a duet: "I told him I'd be delighted," said Joel, "and I invited him round to the studio to share a pizza and some cans of beer. But I guess that was too much for a vegetarian to handle. He didn't show up." But then why should the man who claimed he worked best on his own *care* that nobody ever asked him? "I tried collaborating with somebody once but it doesn't work," he'd once said. "Like I'll write the melody and the other person will come out with these cosmic words like 'Flying through the clouds in a zodiac chariot.' And I don't want to say that."

"I'm so insecure, I sometimes don't know which the real me is," was another thing Billy had once said. But he'd only been talking about music, and how he would change his voice to fit the mood of different songs, about how he admired Paul McCartney "because his

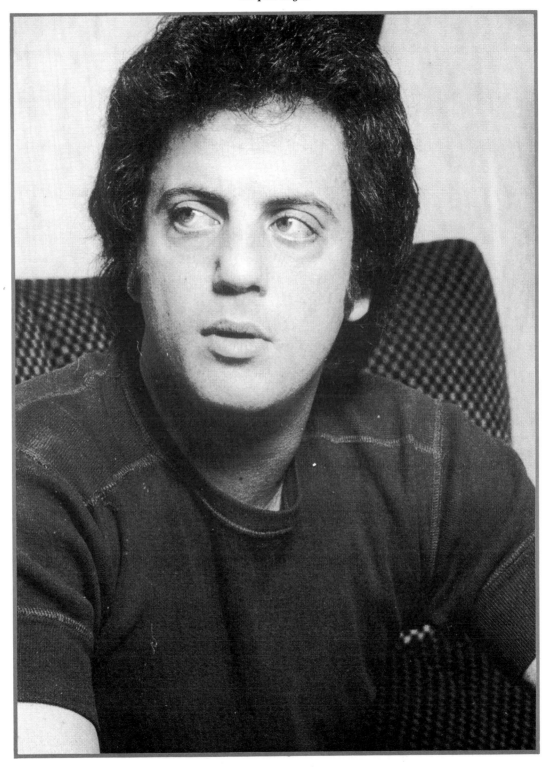

Billy receives his Grammy award in New York, February 1981

voice can pull off these real dopey records," about how he smoked a pack or so of Camel or Marlboro cigarettes a day in an attempt to rough up his tubes so he'd sing like Ray Charles. Away from music, Billy Joel rarely admitted to feelings of insecurity; yes, he'd felt like topping himself back in 1970, but *now:* "I just sit back and let life whack me around. I've got my feet ready to punch. I'm *planted*." And during the early months of 1982, while Joel worked on a studio follow-up album to *Glass Houses,* life decided to whack him around some more, delivering a few telling blows to mind and body.

"You're always in the desert looking for the oasis and all that's out there with you is the piano – this big black beast with 88 teeth . . . 50,000 packs of cigarettes later, you start getting it."

His partnership, marital and professional, with Elizabeth was turning sour. "When Elizabeth and I got together, I wanted it to be forever. I bought that dream." But after ten years, the dream was wobbling into reality and, in the summer, the couple would divorce. And before that, in the spring, in the afternoon of April 15, Billy Joel crashed his Harley Davidson, and the accident almost finished off Billy Joel, recording artiste, for good.

He'd just had his motorbike serviced and was taking it out for a Long Island spin. It was running like a top. Until, at an intersection, a lady in a car shot a red light: "She zoomed through the intersection and there she was. There was no time to do anything." Billy's bike hit the car, flipped right over the top and Billy landed in his leathers on the tarmac. "I thought I was going to die and I was pissed off at the car which looked the size of Brooklyn to me. I thought 'You can't do this to me. I'm not ready to die.' " And then he remembered his bike: "I forgot all about dying and thought 'My bike! My bike!' I was so *mad*. I'd just gotten it fixed." He jumped up and

tried to drag the machine out of the intersection; it was then that he noticed his injuries: "My wrist was swelling up like a balloon and junk was hanging out of my thumb." His left wrist was broken, the hand was badly damaged and, just like in some sappy old movie, it seemed as if the boy who lived for his music would never play the violin (or, in this case, the piano) again. Extensive surgery would ensure a (reasonably) happy ending: a metal pin was inserted, temporarily, through the finger knuckles to hold the bones in place and the hand healed quickly. But the thumb remained crooked and stiff and playing those hard, hammered bass notes that had caused piano strings to snap in the past would be a problem from now on.

Recording of the new album had begun in November 1981; with Billy's hand in plaster-cast, it was shelved for six weeks. Even without the accident, the LP was not proving an easy one to create; sometimes writing songs could be a breeze but this time he had to fight with himself and struggle to get them out: "You pace the room with something like the dry heaves, having no control of the muse, horrified that it won't come. You're always in the desert looking for the oasis and all that's out there with you is the piano – this big black beast with 88 teeth. . .50,000 packs of cigarettes later, you start getting it." The album was completed finally in July 1982 and released the following month. And when they heard the finished article, *The Nylon Curtain,* critics were astonished. They had been expecting some wishy-washy formula rock and MOR tinkly-tonkling from the "bland, mellow balladeer with pretensions to rock'n'roll." Instead they found something *serious* and intriguing. This was *au-then-tic* music that justified BJ's arrogance at last; the man had come out fighting and he had produced a peculiar masterwork.

The LP's front cover design alone was enough to suggest that this was no ordinary Billy Joel album: for the first time since *Streetlife Serenade,* and Brian Hagiwara's remarkably unremarkable street-scene painting, Billy himself was nowhere to be seen. Previous cover designs had been composed of photographs of the artiste in stagey poses that, supposedly, made some visual statement about the man and his music: the rock-

Billy receiving his citation from the Mayor of Allentown

Elizabeth Weber Joel and Dr David Andrews hold a press conference in New York following an operation performed on Billy's wrist and hand

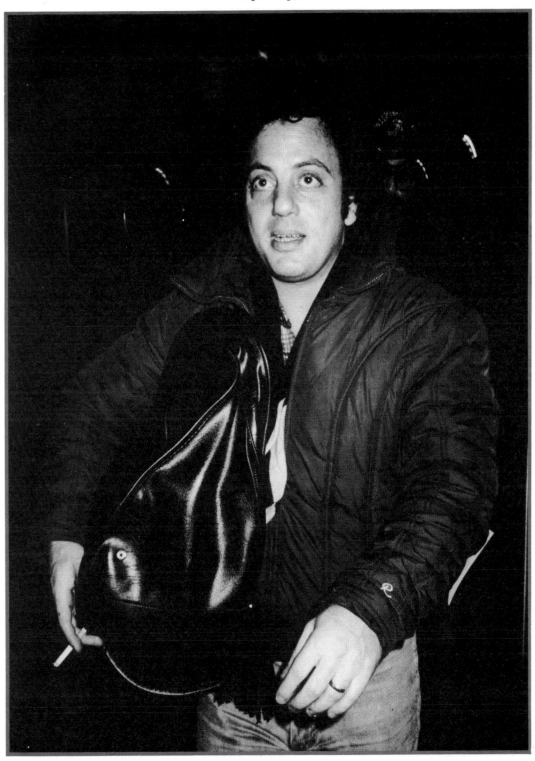

throwing leatherboy of *Glass Houses,* the New York City citizen down in the subway (surrounded by a bunch of New York stereotypes hired from some model agency) of *Turnstiles,* the shadowy figure of *The Stranger* who sat on a bed, between a mask and some boxing gloves, with bare feet – just like McCartney in *Abbey Road* – challenging you not to think "Hey! This is symbolic." (One who rose to this challenge – and got it all hopelessly wrong – was Chuck Marshall who, on his Hollywood radio programme *Rock Around The World* in 1978, had this to say: "With so much gang-related activity in Billy Joel's past, it's no surprise to find Sylvester Stallone, better known as 'Rocky', on the cover of the latest LP, *The Stranger.*" Come again Chuck?) The cover of *The Nylon Curtain* pulled no such stunts; in Chris Austopchki's simple design, large letters announced artist and title and sandwiched between was a row of identical little houses with identical little cars in identical little garages. The "little boxes on the hillside" of suburbia. And on the inner sleeve the little boxes appeared again in an aerial photograph of some anonymous suburb – rows of squat houses stretching on forever. According to Ramone, the album saw Billy Joel speaking up for the people who dwelt there. According to Billy himself: "It's about the stuff people in my age group who grew up as Cold War babies have gone through – our attitudes and our American experience: guilt, pressures, relationships, and the whole Vietnam syndrome."

Elsewhere on the album, Joel turned his attentions to more universally felt subjects such as bad relationships ('A Room Of Our Own'), worse relationships ('Laura') and non-relationships ('Pressure', on which the singer spat upon the shallow values of the cosseted inhabitants of plastic-land, the kind of people who go to "groovy" tap dance classes and trade "Peter Pan advice" and "cosmic rationales"). And then there were personal songs that defied analysis and that Billy himself was reluctant to talk about: "That's one song I'm not even going to attempt to explain," he said of 'Surprises'. "The only thing I can say about that is it's sort of a grand metaphysical statement. We're not really in control of things." Work it out for yourself and, while you're at it, work out 'Scandinavian Skies',

arguably the LP's most outstanding number and similarly hard to pin down. This combined surreal elements borrowed from John Lennon's 'Strawberry Fields Forever' and 'I Am The Walrus' – backwards guitars, mad swooping violins in unexpected quarters, etc – with other insidious aural devices – military snare rattles, orchestral strings and piano men crossing purposes in the middle eight – to create something quite compelling. "It took six weeks to mix," said Billy of 'Scandinavian Skies'. "There were so many different things going on in it. It was like one of those old records where you put on big headphones and plug them into your stereo set and sit in a chair and go 'Oh wooooow!!' And you call up somebody and say 'Did you know there was a banjo way in the background?'" But what was it about? This was the kind of psychedelic swirl that The Hassles had been aiming at – but missing by miles and miles – on *Hour Of The Wolf;* if 'Scandinavian Skies' had been recorded 15 or so years earlier, everyone would have thought the song was about drugs, it sounded so weird and spooky. But this was 1982. And this was Billy Joel. It couldn't be about drugs could it? "Well, it's a little dicey explaining the song. There are drug references in it, put it that way. It's about a pretty gruesome experience. It was a pretty heavy drug." It sounded like it, this piece of modern psychedelic paranoia. On 'Captain Jack', Joel had been the wise observer, saying this is what drugs can do to *you* and it's not very nice. Here he was a decade later saying this is what drugs (a dabble in heroin) once did to *me* and it was bloody horrible. And wasn't I stupid?

Billy Joel had grown up. If there was one criticism of *The Nylon Curtain,* it was that he swiped just a bit too much off The Beatles: 'Laura' was pure Lennon/*Abbey Road* stuff (with pure Harrison/*Abbey Road* guitar solo to boot), while 'A Room Of Our Own' filched more than a little from McCartney's "raunchy" period circa the *White Album.* But so what? If you're going to steal, you may as well go for the best shot. And Billy Joel had carried out this thieving with a lot of class.

The Nylon Curtain was a commercial success (unsurprisingly: the name Billy Joel was guarantee of sales by now); more significantly, it was an "artistic" success. *Rolling Stone* acclaimed it as "Billy Joel's brutally frank . . . pop masterpiece" and the LP was granted (almost) universal admiration.

It had been an exhausting process. "I feel like *The Nylon Curtain* nearly killed me," he had said, and he hadn't just been referring to his accident. The album had been shot through with jolting effects – "aurally ambitious" as *Rolling Stone* said – and getting these just right had been a gruelling slog; never mind composing the *songs,* which had taken so long to form, which had been his most uncompromising musical statements yet – not gloomy for the sake of it but dark at the edges. But he had got it out and he had won through. What more did he have to prove? Damn all, really. Well, there was *one* thing. Would he be able to remain a major commercial contender in the changing, image-obsessed pop climate of the mid-Eighties? The answer to this would be a resounding YES. Almost by accident, determined – after the "heavy trip" of *The Nylon Curtain* – to lighten up and have some fun with the next LP, he would turn himself into an international pop star. Of the millions of pop consumers outside America that were to buy *An Innocent Man,* and the singles drawn from it, many had never even heard of Billy Joel before. All they knew was that the funny-looking man in those videos had some good little pop tunes up his sleeve.

One of the most surprising things about Billy's career in the mid-Eighties is the success he's had with videos, the ubiquitous promotional films that have now become crucial in making or breaking a new band, and seriously challenging established stars' ability to maintain their chart dominance. With the arrival of MTV in the summer of 1981, promotional videos – usually seen in clubs, occasionally on syndicated chart shows – suddenly became *de rigueur* in the marketing of new records. In fact, on the *Billboard* Top 100 charts, there is now an indication beside every record as to the availability of an accompanying video; most Top 30 hits have that little dot beside their title, you can be sure.

The prevailing notion held by industry bigwigs was that videos were going to kill Billy Joel's career, much in the way that many silent stars hit the skids when they were discovered to have squeaky or heavily-accented speaking voices. Billy, they felt, would not look good on video; he's not sexy, in fact many would say he's downright unattractive. He's short, and dark, far from the blonde good looks of boys like Duran Duran and The Fixx whose videos helped skyrocket their dubious recordings to gold status in the US. Nor is Billy flamboyant, like Culture Club or Eurythmics, also champions in the rock video stakes. His straight ahead stage costume is as wild and wacky as jeans, shirt, jacket, tie and sneakers can get you. If the critics couldn't kill Billy, then the man himself, for all 14 million MTV viewers to see, would.

But it didn't happen. Although he doesn't like videos, Billy has become wildly popular as a video star because his videos have been uniformly a cut above the rest, with a warmth, humour and imagination missing in most promos.

Billy's first video, 'Allentown', was directed by Robert Mulcahy and featured Billy as a guitar-strumming balladeer in the tradition of Woody Guthrie. The black-and-white shots of Depression-era railroads, foodlines, and unemployed workers complemented the song perfectly. And Billy's winsomeness impressed many people, including Duran Duran's John Taylor who named 'Allentown' one of his ten favourite videos. The follow-up, 'Pressure', also directed by Mulcahy, was probably Billy's weakest video. Its *Clockwork Orange* posturing, combined with every stupid cliché rock videos have become notorious for – tortured lying in bed, haughty women in the mist, tricks with water and windows – make the video ponderous going. Since Billy is uncomfortable with that kind of affectation, he looks uneasy and a little silly. It's no wonder that he went straight for a more effective presentation on his next video, 'Goodnight Saigon', which showed him singing the song live on a concert stage, a place Billy feels very comfortable. The stage presentation is shown warts and all, with girls in the audience mouthing the words soulfully and passionately. The song is intercut with snapshots from Vietnam: soldiers in their camps and on the battlefield, scenes of death and other wrenching souvenirs of the Vietnam War. When the male chorus, who are meant to seem like the vets themselves, but are actually members of the stage crew, lock arms and sing "We said we would all go down together," it's hard not to hold back the tears. The whole package may avoid some of the greater issues and problems of Vietnam vets, but the song, pictures and chorus vividly recreate the terror and poignancy of the war in Southeast Asia.

When *An Innocent Man* was released in 1983, the video boom was in full swing. Budgets were getting bigger and bigger. Storylines were expanding, and industry faith in the power of video was at its blindest. 'Tell Her About It' featured a guest star, Rodney Dangerfield, whose neurotic, twitchy New York comedy was the perfect counterpart to Billy's music, and a deeply nostalgic setting, *The Ed Sullivan Show*. The video charmingly evoked those Sunday nights when Ed's show signalled the end of the weekend, the last gasp of freedom with big stars to boot. Not only was the video technically extravagant and good fun, it was also the first one where Billy seems to be enjoying himself.

'Uptown Girl' is Billy's most satisfying video. Full of self-references, the video was shot in almost Hopperesque hyper-realism and featured Billy's best dance moves ever.

The last video taken from *Innocent Man*, 'The Longest Time', was another display of Billy's winsome charm. Billy is at a high school reunion where he and the old gang, now pot-bellied and grey-haired, sing some old songs and are transformed to enthusiastic, teenage boys once again.

Billy has released one full-length video, 'Live From Long Island'. Recorded at Nassau Coliseum in December 1982, Billy performed all his hits, including a stirring rendition of 'Piano Man' and a hyped version of 'Scenes From An Italian Restaurant'. Although the show begins with Billy showing restraint at the piano, by the end of the performance he's dancing all over the stage, throwing boxer's jabs and enjoying the enthusiastic home-town crowd. The video has been edited a little clumsily – Billy is very amusing live, but his remarks are unskilfully taken out – nonetheless, the video is an accurate and effective document of Billy's prodigious live talents.

With the complaint being made ad nauseam that video is dehumanizing, forcing viewers to have ideas about songs thrust down their throats and exposing them to the same violent and sexist images, Billy Joel's forays into the field are a welcome relief. They are good-humoured, original, entertaining, and very human, and set Billy apart from the majority of his contemporaries.

DISCOGRAPHY

THE NYLON CURTAIN

(September 1982)

SIDE ONE
Allentown
Laura
Pressure
Goodnight Saigon

SIDE TWO
She's Right On Time
A Room Of Our Own
Surprises
Scandinavian Skies
Where's The Orchestra?

ALL WORDS AND MUSIC: Billy Joel
PRODUCER: Phil Ramone
MUSICIANS: Liberty DeVitto *(drums);* Russell Javors *(guitar);* David Brown *(guitar);* Dominic Cortese *(accordian);* Charles McCracken *(cello);* Eddie Daniels *(sax/clarinet);* Rob Mounsey *(synthesizer).*

SINGLES:
'Pressure';
'Allentown';
'Goodnight Saigon'.

A FOOL FOR LESSER THINGS

Billy and Elizabeth divorced in the summer of 1982, confirming rumours that had been circulating for a year or two about strains in their marriage. Billy was obviously upset about the divorce and reluctant to discuss it, though he did tell *Musician* that touring "may have contributed to the change, but it happened in dribs and drabs, bits and pieces, until we realized we were not together as one, we were together as two." He went on to say: "It's not a Hollywood soap opera. I'm sorry that it had to occur because I'm one of these people who wanted to be married just once and for the rest of my life; one commitment, with one common goal. Our marriage was not something either of us took lightly, and we're both unhappy it didn't work out."

Billy says that the marriage was beginning to fall apart as far back as 1980. As he told

> **❝** *I don't feel that 'I want to be loved by millions because I was deprived as a child' thing. I don't need all that love. Just give me one hell of a good woman. And if I go to the electric chair, that woman's going to love me anyway. 'I killed forty million people and slashed their tongues out and raped most of them. And there's a woman that loves me anyway.' That's what I* **❞** *want.*
>
> **Billy Joel, 1979**

British journalist Simon Kinnersley, it may have been Elizabeth's management of Billy's career, which he reportedly was so pleased with in the beginning, that led to their break-up. "The trouble is that you start discussing business in bed . . . and you're no longer living as husband and wife. And because I'm not business oriented, I'm not really that interested. She started to manage my private life. . . I decide what I'm going to do and what I'm not going to do and no one tells me how I'm going to do things. . . I don't like people who start looking upon me as a product, particularly my wife. . . After a while you find that you don't want to be with that person any more."

Billy relates one post-divorce story which, whether it's true or not, gives a pretty clear insight into the couple's relationship. When Billy played Elizabeth 'Just the Way You

Are', explaining that it was a birthday present for her, she apparently responded: "That's nice. Do I get the publishing?"

Billy insisted that he and Elizabeth would never be completely estranged from each other. "She's a good friend and I hope not to lose that," he explained. "I don't want to fight about the change in our lives or be unnecessarily distant from someone I was married to for nine years and lived with for over eleven . . . I certainly don't have anything bad to say regarding her."

After the couple split, Billy "dated occasionally," but the attachments were never very serious. Friends worried about him, but as he told Chris Connelly: "A lot of people are calling up, going 'Are you going to be OK? Is it lonely?' And I'm like, 'No man. I feel good.' "

Billy felt good enough in January 1983 to take his first vacation in five years and so he flew down to the Caribbean for some R and R. One night he went down to the hotel piano and, in an evening reminiscent of his Executive Lounge days, began playing requests for the assembled guests. One of them was Christie Brinkley. One of the world's most highly paid and recognizable models, Brinkley was particularly well known for her bathing-suit spreads in *Sports Illustrated,* but not only can she command a couple of thousand dollars a day for services, she maintains control over all aspects of her career and spin-off businesses. According to Billy's account of their meeting, Christie and her friends hung around the piano singing along for a while. Afterwards the two began talking to each other; they seemed to be hitting it off, though they didn't really fall in "love" until four months after their first meeting. Billy says: "We started out as friends and then fell in love, which is the best way, rather than crashing in and then the romance burning out after a few months."

Billy has spoken often about Christie's intellectual abilities, but it is her looks that are more obviously arresting to the public. As he puts it, "There's something beyond her looks. She is a very sweet person. She hasn't got that snotty attitude of some models and she's not skinny, she's nicely rounded which is very important in bed." However, Billy says she shares the same confusion about celebrity that he does and their mutual discomfort and

"What's a beautiful woman like Christie doing with me? Well, don't ask me. I haven't a clue. I'm not good-looking. That's not false modesty, it's fact. That I can attract such a beautiful woman as Christie should give hope to every ugly guy in the world."

bewilderment about being constantly in the public eye may be one of the cementing aspects of their relationship.

Christie, for her part, thinks that Billy is "cute". Billy responded to the assessment with convincing modesty, "That's good enough for me. It's good news for guys. . . What's a beautiful woman like Christie doing with me? Well, don't ask me. I haven't a clue. I'm not good-looking. That's not false modesty, it's fact. That I can attract such a beautiful woman as Christie should give hope to every ugly guy in the world – there's hope for them all. If I can do it, so can they. It should cheer everybody up."

One thing is certain, Billy isn't going to ask Christie to manage him. "One thing I have learnt, though," he admitted, "is never make the same mistake twice. However good Christie may be in business, I'm not going to let her manage my career – even though she wouldn't want to anyway – and have the same thing happen all over again."

When the couple announced their engagement in August 1984, the news got a mention in publications all over the world. But unlike many other superstar couples, Billy and Christie don't frequent Limelight or Xenon, attend premières or other society functions. Instead they spend a lot of their time in Long Island at Billy's Oyster Bay home with frequent visits to Hicksville. And when they get away from it all, they're more likely to head for unglamorous Maryland beaches than St Tropez or Martha's Vineyard.

But the most important thing for Billy is that Christie appears to have changed his mind about love and his ability to love, providing the inspiration for *An Innocent*

Man. "It's funny because I really thought that I was so worldly-wise and experienced that I would never *really* fall in love again. After my marriage I did a sort of inventory on myself, and I firmly believed that I wasn't going to fall in love again. That was a phase of my life that had come and was gone for ever. Now I've learnt that you're never too old to fall in love and it can be just as wonderful. . . I've discovered that you can be just as crazy when you're in love in your thirties as you can when you're sixteen.

"On every album I adopt a different sort of character," says Billy, and the character on *An Innocent Man,* released in September 1983, exactly one year after its predecessor, reflected his feelings at the time; this was "sort of a sweet person who is in love and feeling good. . .I wanted to have as much fun as I could have, and I wanted it to *sound* like I was having fun." This time round there was no torturing himself in the struggle with the black beast of 88 teeth, the songs just came spurting out – ten songs in seven weeks, songs that harked back to the soul, R&B and pop music of his youth, the radio sounds of the late Fifties and early Sixties. Another album, another contradiction: seven years before, the man had written 'I Loved These Days' (on *Turnstiles),* partly in reaction to the nostalgia craze – "Everyone was covering old songs and *Happy Days* was a big hit on TV. I was saying 'I *loved* these days but I don't want to go *back* to the Fifties – that's reactionary.' "

Now, in 1983, he *was* going back, reactionary or no. And why not? The "character" on this album was "just a guy enjoying the courtship ritual, making out, dating, slow dancing." And wasn't Billy then enjoying the courtship ritual himself, for the first time in years, with Christie Brinkley? Anyway, it was high time he took a wee trip down memory lane, as they say, and revisited his adolescence: "How can you go through puberty without hearing 'When A Man Loves A Woman' by Percy Sledge?" he asked. "I wanted to hear songs like that on the radio again. So I wrote my own."

The album was the memory of a kid from Hicksville going to his first ever concert and being knocked dead by James Brown and the Famous Flames (a sound recreated on 'Easy Money'), or tuning in to the radio to hear anything from the doo wop revels of Frankie Lymon and the Teenagers or Little Anthony and the Imperials ('This Night'), to the clean-cut boy-next-door twinkling pop of a thousand Neil Sedakas ('Careless Talk'), to the boisterous Latino falsetto romps of The Four Seasons ('Uptown Girl': Billy becomes Frankie Valli to woo Christie). "Back in those days on the radio, you'd have everything. They'd play Peter and Gordon and Wilson Pickett back to back – it was a beautiful pot-pourri of music."

An Innocent Man was a beautiful pot-pourri too. "It doesn't really ape anything," insisted Billy, "it just *feels* like it." It *did* feel like it, and only once – on 'Christie Lee' where Joel tried to do an old-time key-crushing Jerry Lee Lewis-type rock'n'roll "thang" to awkward effect – did his original replays of the musical past fail to hit the mark. From the Philly soul bluster of 'Tell Her About It' to the acapella harmonising of 'The Longest Time', the man seemed to get it just right. (He had little excuse *not* to get the a capella style right, for, he said: "A capella used to be a way of life. We'd cut out of school and hang out on the street corners and polish up the four-part harmony stuff. Or we'd go to the boys' locker-room – that was always good for an echo. The bathroom was a good place too. And there was a beach called Jones Beach in Long Island and there's a parkway there on one side and the beach on the other side and you've got to walk under this long tunnel and it sort of sounds like the Vatican. That was the prime place to do four part harmonies.")

An Innocent Man had captured the lighter side of Joel's youth, even throwing in a bit of Beethoven for good measure (the chorus of 'This Night'), and, on the closing track, 'Keeping The Faith', he set out to justify the whole project, saying "The good old days weren't always so good." In other words, he wasn't simply wallowing in a pink fog of nostalgia – "I'm not living in the past," he said, "I'm celebrating *today*." The public, however, didn't much care what it was he was celebrating, past, present or future; this was simple, satisfying music, innocent and direct pop and that was all that mattered. These

songs required no deep listening process or analysis, you just jigged about to them or got soppy over them. (Probably the only persons who *did* try to analyse a song from the LP were the team behind the BBC World Service radio programme *Pedagogical Pop* on which the lyrics of pop songs are used as English language teaching aids. In November 1984, 'Tell Her About It' went under the programme's microscope and the two presenters, a frightfully jolly and well-spoken couple called Peter and Sue, got quite excited about the inclusion, in the third verse, of the word "insure":

Sue: "If you're driving along in your car and you have an accident. . ."

Peter: "Don't worry! You can *insure* yourself. And your house. And your car. . ."

Sue: "*Insure* them against illness. Or fire. Or loss. . ."

Peter: "Loss of a girl? Perhaps. But even insuring yourself is not a *guarantee* that she won't leave. . ."

Sue: "So. If you want to keep a girl . . ."

Peter: "Tell her about it. . ."

An Innocent Man was an enormous commercial success, not just in America, where success was, of course, expected anyway, but in Europe too. In Britain, up until now, Joel had had a large following and his records had sold healthily, but he'd never been a big league cheese. 'Uptown Girl' changed that; the single went to Number 1 – his first UK Top 10 hit and one of only two million-selling singles in 1983 – and boosted sales of the album which climbed to Number 2. Subsequent singles from the LP – 'Tell Her About It' (a US Number 1), 'An Innocent Man', 'The Longest Time', 'Leave A Tender Moment Alone' – kept him on the charts through the first half of 1984 and in June he arrived, triumphant, to play sell-out concerts at London's vast Wembley arena.

Billy and his band had been playing around the US earlier in the year, and the concerts had been like celebrations: the road crew would celebrate by donning masks and banging assorted bits of percussion on 'Don't Ask Me Why', returning later as greasy, finger-snapping hoodlums for some falsetto loopiness on 'Stiletto'; keyboard player Dave LaBolt would celebrate by tying the star's shoelaces together while he (the star) stood

atop his grand piano saluting his audience, Liberty would celebrate by thrashing his kit to hell, as per usual, and swapping incomprehensible jokes with his boss; and the audience would celebrate by going faintly bananas. No newspapers got ripped to shreds on stage, because none of that really mattered any more. In a career spanning 20 years, Billy Joel had done it all. He'd made a fool of himself. He'd emerged a champion. He'd seen everything in between. What else was there?

He had complained that no one ever invited him to appear on their records. He had wanted to duet with Michael Jackson but little plans had crumbled into nothing. He felt shunned by his popular musical peers. But finally, on January 22 1985, Billy Joel was to join the most prestigious array of American rock talent ever assembled in one recording studio. It was just after the American Music Awards "ceremony" in Los Angeles that 37 of the finest "popsters" in the USA gathered together to record Michael Jackson and Lionel Richie's 'We Are The World', a single that would raise millions of dollars for the starving people of Ethiopia. Bruce Springsteen was there. Bob Dylan was there. Stevie Wonder was there. Paul Simon, Ray Charles, Hall & Oates, Huey Lewis, Cyndi Lauper, Dionne Warwick, Willie Nelson and many more were there. Billy Joel was there. He had two lines to sing: 'And the truth's you know love is' on his own, and then in harmony with the veteran soul queen Tina Turner: 'All we need'. Not much perhaps, but it was worth it. USA For Africa, as the VIP choir was called, went to Number 1 in charts across the globe and even outsold its charitable predecessor, Band Aid's 'Do They Know It's Christmas'.

"It wasn't an ego bath," Billy was to comment afterwards. "It was just spiritually uplifting. I'll tell you, there is nothing like peer recognition. It made up for every bad review I've ever had..."

You could forgive Billy his inactivity during 1985 – he was busy with invitations, caterers, fitters and preachers. And even if Madonna and Sean Penn stole the honors on the cliffs of Malibu later in the summer, on March 23 1985, Billy Joel and Christie Brinkley were married in what was then called "The Rock Wedding of the Year".

Although Billy and Christie were a visible

couple months before the actual event and obviously destined to walk down the aisle together, Billy was constantly having to defend himself to critics who accused him of calculated upward mobility and selling out his Levittown roots. "I'm not marrying this woman because she's a high fashion model," Billy protested, "she's a wonderful person. It bothers me that people think I'm motivated by things like that. I've never sold out." Billy went on to explain that his family also loved Christie and were pleased to see a certain change in his mental and emotional outlook. "They think she's a real sweet person, which she is, who's made me very happy. A lot of people have told me that – that I'm so happy. I feel happy. I must have been a real drag at one time."

About 150 guests – a modest amount considering the bride and groom's high-celebrity profile – received Christie's modest invitation. Once an art student, she had hand-drawn the invitation, a charming sketch of the bride and groom on a boat surrounded by the New York skyline and a sky resplendent with hearts and musical notes. "We've been waiting to do this for the longest time," was the simple message.

The wedding day itself was cold and drizzly, but failed to dampen the spirits of the guests, including Paul Simon, Brian Setzer of the Stray Cats, and Bill Zampino, Billy's first boss and now his best man, as they boarded the 147-foot yacht, the *Riveranda*, draped with a thousand white tulips.

The boat drifted out to the middle of New York harbor, a location chosen as much for its inaccessibility to clamouring reporters as its romance quotient. The bride was elegant and beautiful in a white satin gown designed by Norma Kamali, high-necked and overlaid with ivory lace and gold tulle, the groom quietly suave in a black tuxedo and cummerbund.

Billy was clearly nervous before the ceremony, asking everyone around him, "How do I look?" But there was no sign of pre-vow jitters when Christie joined Billy in front of Judge Shirley Fingerhood and he gave her a long, exuberant kiss.

The ceremony itself lasted a brief seven minutes. Instead of the standard oath uttered at most of these events, Billy and Christie wrote their own vows in which they promised to "honor and respect each other's goals and ambitions." The couple then bear-hugged and walked together to the strains of James Brown's 'I Feel Good'.

The *Riveranda* rounded the tip of Manhattan and set sail for the reception held at a restaurant in the unglamorous Queens. The Joels sat at a table for two, ate some wedding cake, danced to a Strauss waltz and left the party before eleven when the enthusiastic DJ twirled 'Uptown Girl' on the turntable.

During their honeymoon a friend of the couple was asked the tired old question of, "What do they see in each other?" The reply: "She thinks she's marrying a highfalutin' guy while he thinks he's marrying the most beautiful girl in the world. He thinks, 'Wow, Christie Brinkley.' And she thinks, 'I just married Billy Joel. Can you believe it?'" What more could you want?

∽

In London, before his Wembley dates (which, thanks to the modern miracles of "simultaneous live broadcasting", would be seen by millions), the authors asked him the age-old musical question "Where is your head at, and where are you going?" He didn't know. "I have no idea," he said. "I usually don't have any kind of plan, it just sort of pops out. When you start trying to plan your career like Joseph Stalin, you start getting computerised. So, for a while, I'll just be doing some real-life living, kicking back, *not* being on the road, *not* being in the studio, hanging out, going to a bar, drinking a healthy drink or beer or Scotch, and smoking a pack of cigarettes a day. . .I'm *still* trying to screw up my throat so I sound like Ray Charles. Who knows how much longer I'll be able to hit those high notes. . ." And he walked on down the hall. . .

Who *was* that guy?

Oh, just a guy, an ordinary guy.

What did he say?

Oh, he just said "Hi!" And then he said. . .

"Don't take any shit from anybody."

DISCOGRAPHY

AN INNOCENT MAN
(September 1983)

SIDE ONE
Easy Money
An Innocent Man
The Longest Time
This Night
Tell Her About It

SIDE TWO
Uptown Girl
Careless Talk
Christie Lee
Leave A Tender Moment Alone
Keeping The Faith

ALL WORDS AND MUSIC: Billy Joel (except for the chorus for 'This Night': L.V. Beethoven).
PRODUCER: Phil Ramone
MUSICIANS: Liberty DeVitto *(drums);* Doug Stegmeyer *(bass);* Russell Javors/David Brown *(guitars);* Mark Rivera *(sax); with:* Ronnie Cuber/Jon Faddis/David Sanborn/ Joe Shepley/Michael Brecker/John Gatchell *(horns);* Ralph MacDonald *(percussion);* Leon Pendarvis *(organ);* Richard Tee *(piano);* Eric Gale *(guitar);* Toots Thielemans *(harmonica).*

SINGLES:
'Uptown Girl';
'Tell Her About It';
'An Innocent Man';
'The Longest Time';
'Leave A Tender Moment Alone';
'This Night'.

In the 'Uptown Girl' video it is evident that Billy and Christie are in love

Christie Brinkley with Billy's Garden Platinum Ticket

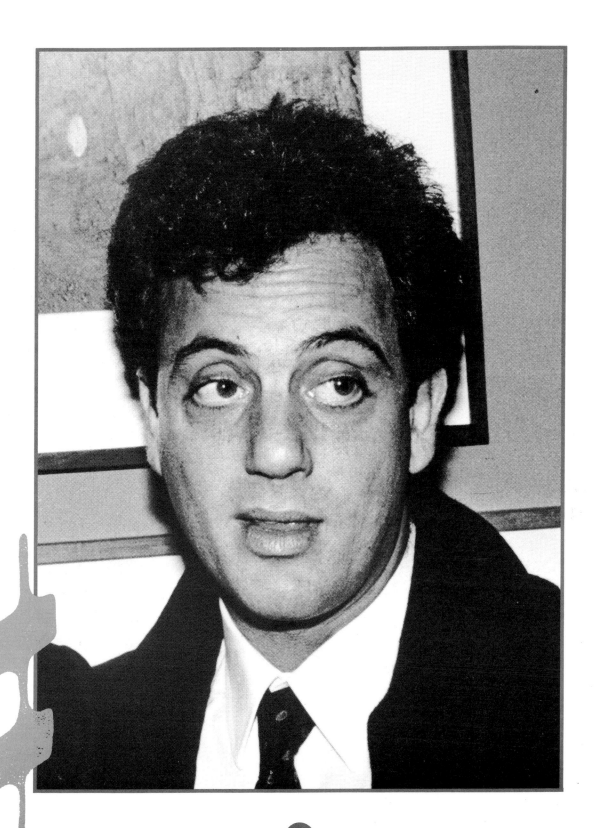

Billy being interviewed for MTV

Billy holds his Madison Square Garden Platinum Ticket, awarded by David A. "Sonny" Werblin, chairman of Madison Square Garden Corporation, presented to music entertainers who have attracted more than 250,000 fans to the Garden